Church Fathers vs. Kingdom Sons

SECOND EDITION

Inheritance Worth Fighting For

CHARLIE COKER

Church Fathers vs. Kingdom Sons: Second Edition
Copyright 2019 by Charlie Coker
First Edition copyright 2013

All rights reserved. No part of this book may be reproduced, stored in a retrieval system, or transmitted in any form or by any means-electronic, mechanical, photocopy, recording, or otherwise-without prior written permission of the copyright owner.

Names of some people in this book have been changed to protect their identity.

Unless otherwise marked, all scripture quotations are from from the *New King James Version*®. Copyright © 1982 by Thomas Nelson. Used by permission. All rights reserved.

Scripture quotations marked (NIV) are taken from the *Holy Bible, New International Version*®, NIV®. Copyright © 1973, 1978, 1984, 2011 by Biblica, Inc.™ Used by permission of Zondervan. All rights reserved worldwide. www.zondervan.com. The "NIV" and "New International Version" are trademarks registered in the United States Patent and Trademark Office by Biblica, Inc.™

Scripture quotations marked "KJV" are taken from the King James Version of the Bible. Public domain in the USA.

ISBN: 978-1-7330786-0-3

Acknowledgments

This book is dedicated to my wife, Susie, who has walked with me, prayed for me, and loved me, in spite of who I was. Your incredible strength and wisdom have shown me a window into God's love that is irreplaceable. I will never forget the day God told me that you didn't decide to stay married to me because of me. It was because you were obedient to and trusted Him. After all I had done to salvage our marriage and family, that was a true kick in the pants! Thanks for loving and trusting God more than you did me.

We are truly blessed to have our sons, Jason and Bryan, in our lives. Thanks, guys, for being patient while Mom and Dad tried to divorce and God wouldn't let us. You guys are the best. Remember the family motto: "If you're going to be dumb, you had better be tough!" Love you!

I also want to thank my mother, Onalee, my father, Charles Sr., and my three older sisters, Becky, Margaret, and Pam. I know it was hard being raised in a family with the youngest being Mom's favorite. But I pray that you are healed from any rejection you may have felt as a result.

Contents

Foreword by Charles Coker Sr.		9
Foreword by Jack Taylor		13
Preface		15
Introduction		17
Round 1	But, My Father!	23
Round 2	The Place of My Birth	39
Round 3	Living for Jesus, Baptist Style	49
Round 4	Leave Your Father's House	59
Round 5	Surviving the Snakes of Church	75
Round 6	The Word of Faith Church	81
Round 7	Being Sent to a Man, Not a Church	93
Round 8	What Do You Do When Your Reality Check Bounces?	113
Round 9	Who's in Charge: Father? Or Son?	133
Round 10	The Younger Brother!	153
Round 11	Sometimes the Fortune's Not What's inside the Cookie	167
Round 12	Birthing the Church	181
Round 13	You Don't Know Jack, Until You Know Jack	193
Round 14	Multiplication by Death!	211
Round 15	Bringing Heaven to Earth	221
Conclusion	The Power of Redeemed Orphans!	235

Foreword by Charles Coker Sr.

On a hot summer day, my son (the author of this book) asked me to let him take our lawnmower and mow a neighbor's lawn. He was ten years old at the time. I allowed him to do it, and he came home totally wet with sweat. He was holding three dollars in his hand and said, "Daddy, I wish I had all the lawns in the world to mow." This episode pretty much describes his personality and motivational makeup: "Full speed ahead, and damn the torpedoes!" In many cases, it has served him well; however, his book gives an overview of the folly of running from God and leaving Him out of our lives.

In his mid-teen years, we would get in each other's faces about some of his and his friends' shenanigans. Though our discussions would become heated—and, when needed, physical—I would still tell him that I loved him, saying, "You are mine; you are my son. No matter what you do, I still love you!" God is good!

In early 1978, I was sent by the postal service to work in New Orleans, Louisiana. This assignment lasted for several weeks. My grandson was born March 14, 1978. Charles turned nineteen on June 22, and Charles and Susie were married in 1980. In February of 1978, I received a letter from my son. I cherish this letter and I have it in front of me right now as I am writing this. With his permission, I share some of his statements and expressions from his letter.

Dear Father:

Church Fathers vs Kingdom Sons

I am in a private place doing a lot of thinking. I know I am "bull-headed" [his words] and don't always do what you would like me to do. When I was growing up I felt you were too strict and unfair at times. Looking back, I see that I was a problem, or would have been if I had not had a firm hand on my backside. I could have turned out a lot worse. You stood up for what you believed and never gave up. Dad, what I am trying to say is, I love you very much, and I know you are behind me all the way.

Love, your son.

In the 1980s, my son was making a lot of money in the lighting business, and we had good fellowship and good times together as a family. But when he was invited to church, we were mostly ignored. My wife confronted Charles about his ungodly lifestyle, and she got away with it. When I prayed about it, God spoke to me and said, "Stop bugging him. He has his idols. Leave him alone!" So I did for nearly five years, but God led me to pray for my son like Job did. In Job 1:5, Job prayed for his sons and interceded before God on their behalf.

For the last fourteen years of service in the post office, I was in a management position. My job, for the most part, was to see to it that other people did their job in a correct and timely manner. As a deacon in the church, I witnessed many parents cutting their children too much slack and leaving an open door to misbehave, and I realized that it was harmful to the child in the long run. I do not doubt that these life assignments had some effect on how I acted and reacted as a parent and father.

For the past fourteen years, I have ministered in the jail and four prisons. Two of these were maximum-security prisons. There are men in these facilities who will never walk the streets again, but because they have invited Jesus into their lives, they have a life worth living—even in prison. This has been the most satisfying time of my Christian life. I do not throw the church under the bus. It definitely has its place in God's plan.

Charlie Coker

As I am writing this in 2013, my son has matured into a man with a passion to bring healing into the lives of those who are hurting. We are on the same page concerning things that really matter. Believe it or not, I have mellowed out a little!

To God be the glory,

Charles Layton Coker Sr.

Foreword by Jack Taylor

Charlie Coker became a spiritual son of mine through a series of events that have the rare fragrance of the miraculous. He is one among many sons whom I treasure and trust. Every time I'm with him, I am impressed at the magnitude of the ministry God has given him. Whether I am buying a book or writing an introduction, preface, or foreword, I first lean toward the author. If I find a man of integrity toward his fellow man, a passion toward God, and a pattern of straightforward truth telling, I build on that sure foundation. I find all these qualities in Charlie Coker.

Now to his book with the fetching title, Church Fathers vs. Kingdom Sons. Even if I were a total stranger to this manuscript and only faintly acquainted with Charlie, my curiosity would have been captured. My deepening acquaintance with the author serves only to multiply my intrigue. The statements that flank the title are valid additions to the subject matter. Above the title the searching question challenges the reader with the words, "Are You Ready to Rumble?" Below the title identifies the expected result of reading this strategic material: "Inheritance Worth Fighting For."

You, my dear reader, are about to receive a shocking challenge in your life as you engage in kingdom principles with the kingdom's operating system: the Father–Son paradigm. In my humble and decisive opinion, herein lies the problem of the modern church: the absence of kingdom mentality. This volume is not so much a study of the kingdom of God as it is a map of one life under the Holy Spirit's direction which led the seeker into a head-on collision with the eternal kingdom of God. The result: a happy fanatic!

Church Fathers vs Kingdom Sons

It is obvious that Charlie Coker is somewhere between slightly and seriously decisive and hardheaded about everything. No lesson he has learned has come without God's decisive action in his life that speaks of a twelve-pound sledgehammer applied to the forehead just above the eyes and directly between the ears. This amazing story is chronicled in surprisingly easy-to-understand language that sometimes comes through with a mild hint of profanity. The author is not content with just writing something to fill the page, but is only satisfied with saying what he writes in the toughest trappings of bald clarity. The reader is apt to experience a reaction with the thought, "Did I just read what I think I read?" My answer to that query is, "You should have read the original manuscript!" This manuscript required many visits to the etymological washateria (a word-usage laundromat) in order to prevent serious offense to the average reader. The editing of the book sought to take the keen edge off of words that were bound to shock and offend, rather substituting them with more delicate words that still convey the thoughts needed for the occasion.

Charlie Coker is not a seasoned scholar or theologian, but a maturing disciple who is seriously in love with Jesus. He is the kind-of novel thinker who will shake the intelligentsia of the church world—and roughly disturb religion in general! By the way, he is not a poor scholar or a bad theologian!

I predict a wide reading of this volume and, in the wake of its reading, a long line of changed lives, awakened passions, and redirected purposes. I will close my contribution here with, "Attaboy, Charlie. You done good!"

Thanks, Susie, for staying with Charlie when anybody else would have flown the coop. You have trained him well!

— Dr. Jack Taylor
Dimensions Ministries, Melbourne, Florida

Preface

You've picked up this book wondering, "Why is this author picturing the church, the body of Christ, in a boxing match? It doesn't make sense. The church is supposed to be in unity and love everyone."

This is the story of my personal journey from being a spiritual orphan to becoming the begotten, spiritual son of the Most High God. This journey started twenty years ago with my first supernatural encounter with Jesus. As God took me step by step, He taught me what not to do, so I could see clearly what to do. As you progress through this book, I urge you to "do as I say, and not as I do (did)." Following the Kingdom Keys can lead you into sonship and a fresh relationship with the Lord.

As I've traveled along this often-unpaved road, I have observed church fathers (leaders in the churches I attended) and the consequences of them being spiritual orphans. Many church fathers have missed their destinies, never fulfilling all the wonders God has had for them to receive and accomplish, because they never understood His love. They continued in the patterns they learned from those before them. They were sons of their fathers. I've seen that there is no greater sin committed by church leaders than repeating the sin that was committed against them. God holds those in leadership accountable for repeating the sins of their fathers. So the boxing match begins.

You have your own personal journey that you are destined to walk. It is ultimately your choice whether you walk as a church father or a

Church Fathers vs Kingdom Sons

kingdom son. If you choose the way of sonship, there is much from my journey that you can glean and apply to your own life, making your journey easier and quicker. Let's rumble!

Introduction

Wow, what a beautiful day! I'm on my way to Houston, Texas, to spend the weekend with Papa Jack Taylor. My mind is churning, wondering how Jack Taylor and his son Tim will receive me.

Is this "spiritual Sonship" thing really real? I know what the Scriptures say in Malachi 4:5–6: "Behold, I will send you Elijah the prophet before the coming of the great and dreadful day of the Lord. And he will turn the hearts of the fathers to the children, and the hearts of the children to their fathers, lest I come and strike the earth with a curse."

But is it really going to work this time? I was thinking about my father and all the pastors and authorities God had given me to submit to over the years. They had, for the most part, all ended in some kind of disappointment. It started with my own dad, who kept me at arm's length for years before accepting that I "might" be a man of God. It continued with the church fathers who couldn't care less about you if you were not under their authority, building their mountain of influence. It didn't matter if it was God who was moving you to go somewhere else; you became obsolete and discarded.

Then I got the phone call that changed everything. It was my dad, asking me what I was doing and why I was going to Houston. I told him I was on the way to the airport to spend the weekend with Papa Jack.

My father said that he was really thankful that Jack was in my life. "I believe that he is an answer to the prayers I've prayed for years. I desired that you would have somebody of his caliber who would really help you in ministry. I am very thankful, as God has answered my prayers."

As Dad took credit for Jack Taylor coming into my life, this ungodly anger started to erupt on the inside of me. The anger of an orphan, that deep anger that hurts in the gut, the pain deep down inside of me, started coming to the surface. It was anger, resentment, rebellion, and hatred—yes, even hatred. Remember, *hate is what love is not.* This level of dishonor had not been allowed to surface like that in a long time. It came to the forefront of my heart, and it looked very ugly and sinful. All of these emotions rushed to the surface at one time. I've had them before, but I've always suppressed them because I'm a fifty-one-year-old father with two natural sons and several spiritual sons. I'm also a pastor and a traveling minister. "Honor thy father and mother that your days will be long, and all will go well with thee": you know, that commandment stuff. I thanked my dad for the prayers and said I would call him next week.

Why did it make me so angry? Sorry God, I must still have some issue with him taking credit for Jack coming into my life. After all, if he had been the man of God he should have been, I would not have needed Jack Taylor.

Learning to Lean

As we arrived in Houston, I met up with a friend who is one Leif Hetland's spiritual sons. Leif was putting on the conference. After we got settled in at our hotel, I called Jack about supper and the meeting arrangements for the night. Leif, Jack, and others of high regard in the Christian community were the speakers that weekend. Here was my prayer for the weekend: "Dear Lord, give me favor with Jack and others. Please help me not to be an embarrassment to Jack or to You. Help me speak with wisdom and grace, and not look like the dumb redneck I feel like most of the time."

The first night Jack spoke, he introduced me to the crowd and told them I was one of his newest spiritual sons. He gave a favorable review

Introduction

of how we'd met and that I was one of his "stranger" sons with the gifting I carry. With that public affirmation after he spoke, he called Tim, Leif, Kris Vallotton, and me to the front to pray for people. As I looked at the crowd, I saw there were as many people wanting prayer from me as the others. I looked at the people lined up in front of me for prayer, and I heard the Lord speak: "This is your inheritance. Welcome to Sonship. Now pray with the authority of heaven."

As we were finishing the evening, we made plans for the next day. We looked at Jack's speaking schedule. He told me that there was a workshop at the same time as when he was speaking and that he wanted me to go learn how to SOAK. I said, "I don't soak." Jack answered, "I know. That's the problem!" I tried to debate, but that didn't work to my advantage at all. Whining and trying to work my way out of it didn't help. I hate to lean back or lie down, and soaking is for sissies!

Jack told me that I needed to learn to lean back. There he goes again! That's all he ever says: "Lean back." That's all he has said to me in over a year of this fathering stuff. I have waited for some correction, great wisdom, or even discipline: a little spanking to straighten me out. All he has ever said is, "Learn to lean back." I don't lean back! Jack shot back, "That's my point, son; that's my point."

I fretted all night. I really wanted to hear Jack speak and didn't like the soaking part. After I did my morning prayers, I got a new attitude and went to the soaking class. People were coming into the meeting room with pillows and blankets. I saw one lady dressed in what looked like her pajamas. But with further investigation, I realized it was just one ugly dress. I figured I had to behave and be a good little boy.

Exposing the Anger

Well, the teaching was okay. Then we had a prayer and they put on some Indian flute, "smoke a joint," music. I found a place in the corner and lay down to soak. Why don't they call it marinating, or pickling, or being in His presence? We called it "sloaking" because it was okay to sleep or meditate. As I got into the presence of God, I heard Him ask, "Why are you so angry with your father?"

I cried out, "Because he tried to take credit for my spiritual success, and he isn't spiritual enough to recognize what You even promised me in 1996 when You took me in a vision. In that vision, I saw my mother at fourteen years old walking up a hill, praying about a coming revival where the glory comes and masses of people get saved and healed. You promised me a Harley and a Rolex watch as gifts to be signs of this coming move of Your Spirit. You said that you would give them to me as signs of the timing of this revival.

"That very Rolex was the same watch that Leif has, and he was the one connected to Jack Taylor. I have never been able to please my dad when it is a spiritual matter, but when I have a little success he takes credit. He doesn't even know that the mantle of the prophet that I walk in was from Grandpa. If Dad had been willing to pay the price, he could have been a giant in the faith. When it comes to spiritual things, he doesn't have a clue. I believe he's ashamed of me, and now he's trying to take credit. I'm ticked!

"You promised seven years ago that Jack would be a father to me, before You moved me into my ministry. How could my father try to take credit for that, just because he prayed some namby-pamby prayer? If he had been the man of God he was supposed to be, I would not have needed Jack Taylor. It has been my obedience to You that brought Jack Taylor into my life. And it makes me mad that after all these years he is trying to take the credit."

The Holy Spirit spoke sternly, "Even after last night's validation in Sonship, you still think like an orphan." He went on, "Charlie, if I had wanted Moses to be the only one delivered from Egypt, I would have never hardened Pharaoh's heart ten times. But I wanted to deliver Moses and the whole nation. That's why I hardened all these men's hearts against you. They weren't capable of fathering you. I would not allow them access to that area in your life."

Introduction

"Even my father?"

"Yes, even your father."

"But why, Lord?"

"If I had allowed them, they would have molded you into their image and not mine. Therefore, I left you an orphan till this season, to bring healing and deliverance to the fatherless in this nation." With that, I went into a vision and saw a list with my dad and nine other leaders to whom I had submitted.

Boxing Time

The Holy Spirit told me to let go of my bitterness and anger because the men had been held back by God and weren't capable of fathering me in the last season. As I started repenting for my resentments and anger, the Lord started speaking to me about those who hurt and how much they need deliverance and healing from the orphan spirit. He asked if I were up to the task of bringing healing to the body of Christ in this area.

As I answered the call, I saw a vision of a gym full of boxers in training. Two boxers were sparring in the ring; others were working out all over in different stations. Some were working the speed bag, some were hitting the heavy bag, and others were jumping rope. As I looked on the wall, I saw a poster of an upcoming main event that read "Church Fathers vs. Kingdom Sons."

Are you ready to rumble?

Author's Note: Some men in this book have served as mentors to me, yet were not my spiritual fathers. Those men will be noted by a double asterisk: **.

Round 1

But, My Father!

Lord, I'm still feeling raw and a little angry on the inside about You hardening the hearts of all these leaders I had submitted to in ministry. That explains why the relationships only went so far. But, God, this isn't fair. I know the answer to that question: "Well, son, tell Me what was fair about the cross they crucified Me on. Still like singing that song, 'I want to be more like You, Jesus'?" It still isn't fair! I am starting to get the meaning of the word my mother gave me on her deathbed.

My mother called me to her sickbed three weeks before she died in 1997. I remember the call at the office. She asked me to drive to Sarasota, where she was to have heart surgery in a few days. She told me that she wanted to see me alone, and to come in the morning.

After I hung up the phone, I went into a vision. I saw my father as the head of the family and that all four of us kids were under his blessing. Then I saw the patriarchal position of my father being lowered as I was being promoted to that position. I asked the Lord, "What does this mean?" He said, "There is an authority shift coming to your family."

I didn't see my mother in the vision, and I asked the Lord, "Is it her time?" I asked if my father was going to die also.

God told me, "No, he isn't."

I asked, "How can I walk in this position of patriarch when my father is still alive?"

The Lord told me that this would only work within the realm of the kingdom and in surrendered vessels.

The Fat Preacher

The next day, I went to see Mom, and she began the conversation. "Charlie, I took a walk with Jesus the other night. We were walking in heaven. We stopped and looked over a balcony, and He showed me your life. I know who you are and I saw your calling." She said, "Your father is a good man, and a man of faith, but not a man of the Spirit. [That is, of the kingdom.] If you let him, he will destroy the gift of God that is on your life. This is your test, not his; but when you prove to him it's from God, he will serve you."

She went on. "Listen to me carefully. If you fail this test, God will not use you in the ministry you have been called to." Then she finished: "You must learn to do war with honor, or you will fail."

My mother's heart surgery was a few days later, and then she suffered a stroke that left her without the ability to speak. During the next three weeks of recovery, she never spoke a clear word to us. The doctors released her to travel across the state back to Vero Beach to a rehab hospital. I let my sister use my Lincoln Town Car so the ride would be more comfortable for my mother, and I drove to Vero to meet them.

I got there and waited on the street corner; my mother, who had not spoken during those three weeks, saw me standing there on the sidewalk. She looked at my sister and said, clear as a bell, "That boy is going to be a fat preacher. Tell him no one listens to a fat preacher, and tell him I said to lose some weight!" My sister was shocked to hear her speak. We all thought that it was funny, and now we have yet another family story. Mom died the next day.

Round 1: But, My Father!

Starting the Journey

Let's take a look at the journey God has had me on. He's teaching me to stop thinking and acting like an orphan and start thinking like a Son and manifest the kingdom. "Lord, my journey has been hard! I know what You said years ago when I asked for a spiritual father. You said no. You had that lady give me Scriptures about the anointing teaching me all things, First John 2:27: 'But the anointing which you have received from Him abides in you, and you do not need that anyone teach you; but as the same anointing teaches you concerning all things, and is true, and is not a lie, and just as it has taught you, you will abide in Him.'

"You told me that You would not allow others to make it easy on me because the day would come when You would send people who, if they listened, would learn from my teachings: what took me years, they would do in months; and what took me months, they would do in weeks; and what took me weeks, they could do in days. The power of my blessing would be an impartation of grace in their lives, and they would get heaven from the laying on of hands.

"But, my father! Why did you list him with all of those leaders that you had me submit to in ministry? Dad was never a pastor. He was always a deacon, Sunday school teacher, and song leader, while Mom played the piano. My dad was a good father in the natural, but wasn't a man of the Spirit; he was incapable of fulfilling the role of my spiritual father in the kingdom. He could only be my mentor."

I remember that when there was a major problem in the church, Dad** and my four spiritual uncles (deacons) would have meetings at the church. Within a few weeks, the pastor would resign or the board would call a membership meeting, and the whole church would have what they called a vote of confidence. Sometimes the pastor would stay, and other times he would leave.

Character is the person you are in the dark when no one else is watching but God. I saw this with my father late one night when I came into the living room to find him praying. I just stood still and listened to him pray. He asked God to help him do what was right. He was willing to keep his opinions to himself, but he needed help doing what was right. This has always had an impact on me, yet he didn't even know I was there. My father always tried to make righteous stands, even if it cost him.

> **Character is the person you are in the dark when no one else is watching but God.**

Spiritual leadership should start in the home. My father was a leader in the church and lived by those rules. He governed his home with the same iron hand that the church used. Yes, there were rules, but there was always a loving side too.

Well, if you haven't figured it out by now, I have a strong personality and God needed to deal with my rebellion. I was raised in the church, so I was saved at a very young age. We will review some of that later.

The Power of a Praying Wife

I still remember at the age of nineteen, I took a walk with my father. We talked about the bleeding ulcers that I was having and that I wanted to join the army. You see, I had fathered a child and denied that he was mine. I was lying about the girl and running from God. Well, the girl, Susie, is now my wife of thirty-two years. (She won; her prayers worked!)

Instead of calling the police and having me arrested for date rape, she started praying. Her mom and my mom were praying together, and I was under so much conviction that I suffered from those bleeding ulcers. I let my father know that the doctor was going to put me on a baby food diet and that if the bleeding didn't stop, they were going to have to operate. Dad looked at me and flat-out told me, "It's not what you're eating, son; it's what's eating you. If you run from responsibility,

Round 1: But, My Father!

you will be running for the rest of your life." At that moment, the Holy Spirit came on me, and I repented and asked Jesus to clean my heart. I made it right with Susie, and within six months we were married.

We started off strong in the church as a new family, and all was well until we had a church problem. The youth pastor was having an affair with someone, and then my cousin felt like leadership had wronged him. So I took up an offense for my cousin. I used it as an excuse to leave the church and all of its garbage. We lasted as a church family for about three years before I slowly became a reprobate. At the same time, I was starting to become successful in business. But, other spiritual wounds—from being held at knifepoint and sexually abused at the age of seven—started coming to the surface.

A deacon's seventeen-year-old son, who later killed two women and died on death row, abused me. Because of my unhealed wounds, I became addicted to pornography and committed adultery. Alcohol was starting to control areas of my life too. Basically, my life was coming apart at the seams. My mother came to my business one day and said that she wanted to talk to my checkbook. She began to tell my checkbook that its owner was a sinful man and there was a call of God on his life.

She looked at me and said, "Every day of your life, I have prayed that the blessings of God would overtake you. I have prayed in every dime and every dollar you have made. But you have turned your heart from God. He has promised me that you would fulfill your calling. And today I made a deal with God. I gave God permission to do whatever it takes for you to get into heaven. He could even kill you, if need be, because you're an adulterer, you're addicted to pornography, and you're a cheat." She pointed at me. "You are a liar. You are not worthy be a husband or a father." She gave me a strong look and told me I had better repent and get right with God. Then she closed the office door and left.

About two minutes later, she came back in and said, "By the way, I love Jesus more than I love you. I will see you in heaven. You can make it easy, or you can make it hard. The choice is yours to make." Well, you would think that would have gotten my attention, but I only hardened my heart more.

The wife, who had prayed for me and believed God's promises, was starting to have her own spiritual crisis. The pornography and her wounds from having been date raped by me were an open door for the enemy to take her out. She started having her own relationships outside our marriage, and we were on a downward spiral. We both had been raised in the church and both knew the truth about God and His ways. Sin has a way of taking you farther than you want to go, keeping you longer than you want to stay, making you do what you swore you would never do, and making you pay more than you want to pay.

> **Sin has a way of taking you farther than you want to go, keeping you longer than you want to stay, making you do what you swore you would never do, and making you pay more than you want to pay.**

Spiritual Cycles

I have found in my life in the kingdom there have been spiritual cycles of three and a half years; some I have passed, and some I have had to retake three to three and a half years later. At the three-year mark of our marriage, we failed the test and left the church system. Seven years after that—two cycles of three and a half years later—my mother spoke judgment over me. Later, my wife of thirteen years moved out. We were heading for divorce. She was so hurt and wounded, and she left both boys with me. I was at the end of my rope.

On August 30, 1993, at 2:30 a.m., I knelt down beside my pool table and prayed this prayer: "God, if you are the God of my mother, a supernatural God; if You're that God, the one who she says has the **power** to change a man's heart; if You are that God, I will give You

Round 1: But, My Father!

a chance to change me. I will not make promises anymore without a change in my heart because I am a liar, a thief, and a whoremonger. I am evil to the core of my heart, and if You can't change my heart, I will never be able to serve You."

As I stood up, I waited for God to say or do something. "Boy," I said, "that was the most honest prayer I have ever prayed." As I started to leave the room, suddenly lightning went off in the room. It was the brightest light I had ever seen!

Out from the light walked Jesus. His eyes pierced my soul. He held out His hand and started to move in my direction. As He stretched His hand to me, He spoke. "Charlie, tonight you choose who you will serve! If you put your hand in My hand, I will never leave you or forsake you. But if you don't choose Me," He pointed and said, "I will let hell have its way with you."

As he pointed, I saw hell open up. I heard the screams, I smelled the reek of sulfur, and I was petrified. At that moment in time, I surrendered 100 percent to the Lord Jesus Christ. He had become my King, Lord, and Savior. Like I had a choice! Sweet little baby Jesus in the manger had grown up and was going to let hell have its way with me. My reality check had just bounced. I had met the King of a kingdom!

(I have always understood the blood covenant that Jesus made on the cross. But this relationship took on a different reality: He had intentions of shedding my blood if I didn't obey Him! Several years later, I asked Jesus why He manifested to me in that way that night. I thought I was something special and waited for the answer. He told me it had little to do with me. He said, "I had your mother in my face day and night, holding me accountable to the promises I made to her about you. And that's what moved me to visit you.")

He asked me if He could use me to bring change to His church. I started to argue that I didn't like His church ... filled with hypocrites. I pleaded with Him, "Please, I have fallen in love with You. I see a King who has a kingdom that is bigger than the mean church system. Please don't make me go there; they have hurt me, and they are mean."

He then said, "Charlie, you're talking about My bride." He continued, "You can't bring change by standing on the outside shooting at it. You have to be on the inside to bring change." He said that He was going to bring me to a place of maturity. In that maturity, I could rebel against the church system I was told to submit to and yet still walk in love. "THIS will bring the change from church to kingdom."

He spoke further: "Follow My examples in My Word. I was part of the religious system of my day, then one day the Father said, 'It is time to release present-day truth for all to hear.'" This was the beginning of *Church Fathers vs. Kingdom Sons* for me. But as the rumbling started, so did the miracles, and the kingdom was advanced as the King was revealed.

That same night Jesus showed me two visions: one of twenty couples in a marriage ceremony with Susie and me among them, and another where I was on stage with thousands, sharing the goodness of my God and preaching the gospel. It took God eleven months to fulfill these two visions. These visions helped me have faith to believe God was going to heal us, so they were important keys to the restoration of my marriage with Susie.

Entering the Kingdom

Many people ask, "How long have you been saved?" Most of the time, I say since August 30, 1993, but the truth is that I had given my heart to Jesus at about five years old. At the age of nine, I had a visitation from the Lord and received the baptism of the Holy Ghost with the evidence of speaking in tongues. In this encounter, I also saw that I was going to preach to masses of black people and came to the conclusion that I was going to be a missionary to Africa.

We had a missionary from Africa visit the church, and when he asked for commitments, I went to the front for prayer about the mission

Round 1: But, My Father!

field. Truth be known, I felt I was born again and had eternal life. Even though I became a racist and was a reprobate in many other areas of my life, God had a plan and was not going to let me go. As the Word says in John 3:1–3 (KJV):

> "There was a man of the Pharisees, named Nicodemus, a ruler of the Jews: The same came to Jesus by night, and said unto him, Rabbi, we know that thou art a teacher come from God: for no man can do these miracles that thou doest, except God be with him. Jesus answered and said unto him, Verily, verily, I say unto thee, except a man be born again, *he cannot see the kingdom of God*" (emphasis added).

Nicodemus was a leader of the religious church of His day. He came to Jesus, who affirmed that God was with Him by the miracles that followed Him. Nicodemus was asking, "What must I do to have the same thing You have?"

This is all about a King who lives in the spirit realm and His kingdom.

I believe that I was born again but was unwilling to pay the price to enter the kingdom realm in which I live today. I feel there are many leaders in the church who love God and are born again but have only been able to see the kingdom and are unwilling to enter into it. Therefore, we have many CEOs running orphanages as leaders in the church today.

On this extraordinary night in 1993, the King of the kingdom got my complete heart, and I entered into the kingdom. I called my dad and asked if he could bring me a Bible. I was so ashamed that I could not find a Bible in my house to wake up with. He showed up at about 4:00 a.m. I asked him if he would drop a duffel bag full of pornography off at the dump on his way home. He began to understand that something had changed that night!

Three days later, I was working on one of our rentals. The tenant had moved out, and I was checking on the place. He had left some alcohol in the bottom cabinet of the kitchen. While I was cleaning it out, a very large, ruler-level demon attacked me. Look, this demon was huge! It started off as very beautiful, and at first I thought it was from God. But when I shouted the name "Jesus!" this thing started hitting me and trying to kill me!

I took the alcohol out on the back porch and started breaking the bottles in a recycling bin. The thing was still trying to kill me! So I started screaming at the top of my lungs, "Jesus, Jesus, the blood of Jesus is against you. Satan, the blood of Jesus rebukes you." I remembered a childhood Bible story where the demons were cast out of a man and into the pigs. They ran into the water and drowned. I figured out that demons couldn't swim, so I jumped into my pool. Each time I would go under the water, the torment would subside, and I could think and pray. I would come up for air and rebuke the devil.

To make a long story short, the cops came and took me to the hospital, where I was strapped to a gurney and asked questions about this demon I had seen. I was arguing about the big old demon that was trying to kill me. Then I heard the voice of my King: "Charlie, settle down. It's going to be okay. I am with you! It's going to be okay." Peace like a river flooded my emotions, and the Holy Spirit started giving me the words to answer the questions that the doctors were asking.

I have shared all of this testimony to get to this part of God bringing healing and deliverance to me.

Submitting to Authority

After a few hours, my father came to see me. As he stood at the foot of the bed, he started to tell me that he wanted me to sign some papers that would voluntarily "Baker Act" me. (This is a commitment to a mental health facility, done either voluntarily or by legal action.) As he asked me to sign them, I started to explain that it was only a demon. I had proclaimed the name of Jesus and pleaded the pure, sinless blood of Christ, so the demon had to flee. I started to argue with him. He

Round 1: But, My Father!

explained that voluntarily signing the papers would be better than if they forced a Baker Act.

"Dad, just take me home to your house and everything will be all right," I said, but he still would not give in to my way of thinking. I started to get angry with him, but then I heard the words of my new King. "For once in your life, do what your authority tells you to do. And do it with the right attitude!"

This was God telling me that never in my whole life had I submitted to authority. He said for "once in your life." I was thirty-three years old and still dealing with rebellion.

I looked at my father and said, "Dad, I think you're wrong in what you have asked me to do, but because you are my authority I will do it. Sorry for the attitude. *Please forgive me*."

At the very moment the word "forgive" came out of my mouth, the Holy Spirit reached into my heart and ripped rebellion right out of me. I felt it come out of my soul and my spirit. This was the beginning of my deliverances from the demonic spirits that I had allowed into my life. At that very moment, the Lord started speaking to me about His plans for my life, and He began to show me that submitting to authority was an absolute MUST to be successful in life and ministry.

The second important kingdom principle God showed me was that authority must start first with me, then with my family.

Within seven days, the Lord brought much healing and deliverance. He dealt with my rebellion against my father and started to rebuild me as a man so He could trust me with my wife.

So my father was the first spiritual authority to whom I had to submit. That was the first kingdom principle God showed me. The second important kingdom principle God showed me was that authority must start first with me, then with my family.

Taking Responsibility for the Family

I had just had a heart change and fallen in love with Susie like never before. But we had lived a lifestyle that was ungodly to say the least.

Susie was having relationships outside of our marriage that were hurting me, and the enemy was still influencing me. One night I made a plan and borrowed a friend's car. I walked a few blocks from the beach and, at one thirty in the morning, was sitting outside the window of the house where Susie and her date were doing the nasty. I sat there with a .44 Magnum, intent on scaring this guy from my wife and, if necessary, killing him.

Then I heard the voice of my new King: "It is your fault that she is sleeping with this man. I do not hold this sin against her; I hold it against you. This is your fault."

How could this be? She's inside this guy's house, and it's *my* fault?

I knew this voice was the voice of my new King, so I left and returned home to pray. I asked the Lord, "How can this be my fault? Your word is very clear, and what she is doing is sin. If this is my fault, can you prove it in Scripture?"

Well, the Lord said, "Glad you asked. Go to Hosea 4:6. 'My people are destroyed for lack of knowledge. Because you have rejected knowledge, I also will reject you from being priest for Me; because you have forgotten the law of your God, I also will forget your children.'"

Then He spoke to me, "If you're going to be a priest for Me, I will give you knowledge on how to bring the proper sacrifice that I require in every arena of authority where I will put you. The man is the priest of his home. Follow My principles and I will help you recover not only your wife, but also your children."

Round 1: But, My Father!

Then verses 12 to 14 jumped off the page (KJV):

> People ask counsel at their stocks, and their staff declareth unto them: for the spirit of whoredoms hath caused them to err, and they have gone a whoring from under their God. They sacrifice upon the tops of the mountains, and burn incense upon the hills, under oaks and poplars and elms, because the shadow thereof is good: therefore your daughters shall commit whoredom, and your spouses shall commit adultery. I will not punish your daughters when they commit whoredom, nor your spouses when they commit adultery: for "*the men*" themselves are separated with whores, and they sacrifice with harlots: therefore the people that doth not understand shall fall.

Armed with this Scripture, I then asked, "What do I do?" The Holy Spirit started giving me words to pray. *I* was responsible for the condition of my marriage and my home! Therefore I stood in my place of authority and repented for my sins and the sins that my wife was committing. That night I started to walk in the authority of the kingdom with my new King.

If you can't rule yourself, you will be disqualified from ruling in other areas.

I remember when my father told me that my wife was making a mockery of me and I needed to get real about my marriage. "It's over, son. You're going to have to face the reality that she doesn't want to be married to you."

I told him, "I understand why you are saying what you're saying, but God promised to restore my marriage. He called her a godly woman full of faith, and He is going to heal her from the inside out. If you can't believe that God can and will heal my marriage and walk with me, I will never talk about it with you again."

My father looked at me and said, "Okay, I will believe with you."

This was a very hard time for me personally, but I very much needed training for the reigning and ruling He was trying to teach me. If you can't rule yourself, you will be disqualified from ruling in other areas.

Choosing Holiness

Susie had moved out, and I was trying to live a holy lifestyle. But remembering the years of pornography and sexual addition was driving me crazy. One night I was in the shower, hornier than a three-balled billy goat, and cried out to God for help. The Holy Spirit told me, "I cannot help you with your problem because it was your actions that put this area out of balance." He continued, "Until you surrender the sexual part of your life to Me completely and offer it to Me as a sacrifice, I will not help You."

So I knelt down and made a personal altar in the shower. I presented that sexual part of my life completely to the lordship of Jesus Christ. The pressure was replaced with peace and power, and I felt His presence at a greater level.

> **Kingdom Key: When His presence becomes more valuable than my pleasure, I will walk in peace and power!**

I walked out of the shower and was drying off when Jesus walked into the room. He had a robe in His hand. He said, "Because you have chosen to walk in holiness, you will need My robe of righteousness to wear." He put a beautiful white robe around me and gave me instructions to write this quote on a 3 x 5 card and read it every day till my mind was

Round 1: But, My Father!

renewed. So I started every day for years with this: "Charles L. Coker Jr. is as righteous as Jesus Christ is because He gave me His robe to wear. I can do what He did and greater."

Kingdom Key: Righteousness is a gift from Jesus! Holiness is a choice to empower righteousness.

After God showed me that He was going to heal my marriage, I had a "come to Jesus" meeting with Him about in my weaknesses in this area. I had truly fallen in love with Susie, but I had to be honest—whether it was six months or five years, I was afraid that I would cheat on her and hurt her again. So I told Jesus that I wanted Him to release Susie from the marriage so she could find a good husband who would not cheat on her.

After three days of talking to the Lord about this, He came to me and asked one more time if cheating was truly the only fear that was holding me back from the healing of my marriage.

He asked me, "If I guarantee that you will never touch another woman inappropriately, do you want Me to heal your marriage?" I asked, "Could you do that?" He said, "I am God. Yes, I can!"

I told God if He would guarantee me that, I wanted my marriage restored.

He then told me to stand on my Bible. As I stood on my Bible, He audibly spoke these words: "Charles Layton Coker Jr., if you ever touch another woman inappropriately, I will KILL you stone dead!"

He took care of that little lust problem in short order!

(In our upcoming book, *From Rape to Righteousness: Redeeming the Bride of Christ*, we will get into more detail about how God has healed Susie and me in this area of our lives.)

Church Fathers vs Kingdom Sons

Lessons I have learned can be found in Galatians 4:1–2: "Now I say that the heir, as long as he is a child, does not differ at all from a slave, though he is master of all, but is under guardians and stewards until the time appointed by the father."

Over the next few years, God taught me how to submit to authority. And this kingdom revelation continued living on the inside of me.

***

Kingdom Keys:

1. The kingdom operates under authority.
2. The King (Jesus) was under authority till the appointed time. (See Galatians 4:1–7.)
3. The kingdom has different levels of authority.
4. When His presence becomes more valuable than my pleasure, I will walk in peace and power!
5. Righteousness is a gift from Jesus! Holiness is a choice to empower righteousness.

Round 2

The Place of My Birth

> And He has made from one blood every nation of men to dwell on all the face of the earth, and has determined their preappointed times and the boundaries of their dwelling (Acts 17:26).

I was puzzled about why Pastor Jimmy** of Central Assembly in Vero Beach was one of the leaders whose heart God had hardened so much that he was unable to father me. I was only submitted to him for about six weeks. I would find out why years later.

After the incredible life-changing experience with Jesus telling me to put my hand in His hand or He was going to let hell have its way with me, and after the revelation that He loved me enough to put my natural life on the line, the Lord showed me that His judgment was one of both love and mercy. Not wrath or death. It was to Live and Love.

He knew what it would take to complete that task! The supernatural power of God changed my heart of stone into a heart of flesh. The supernatural was a demand for change, and it was the only way I could have followed Him. I believe the power of the supernatural is the key to a revival being sustained that will change the culture of our nation.

When a friend tells you to go to hell, it only hurts; but when Jesus, the one who holds life and death in His hands, tells you to go to hell, that's a different story. Jesus certainly had this redneck's attention:

Church Fathers vs Kingdom Sons

The fear of the Lord is the beginning of wisdom: a good understanding have all they that do his commandments: his praise endureth forever (Psalm 111:10 KJV).

I believe the power of the supernatural is the key to a revival being sustained that will change the culture of our nation.

Proof of a Changed Life

He spoke to me about getting involved with the local church. He said that I couldn't bring change by shooting from the outside, but by being involved. One of my lifelong friends who was instrumental in my conversion, Tim Bishop, was going to Central. Tim tells the story like this. (Tim and I were friends all through high school, so you know we got into a lot of trouble with car racing and girl chasing, to name just a few of our sports.)

Tim got saved about a year before I had my encounter with Jesus. He worked for UPS and would eat lunch in my office at the lighting store. So, I had to hear about his new life with Jesus. Tim was not from a religious family, so all this Jesus stuff was fresh to him. After about eight months of him witnessing to me, he started pushing my buttons and asking questions like, "Charlie, how can a person who was raised in church like you ignore the truth and live the way you're living?" The smoke would roll out of my ears.

With my church background, I gave him an earful. I started hating him with a demonic passion. Tim lived in my neighborhood, and as my family and I went to take the boat out on Sundays, we would pass by his house while his nice little Christian family was going to church. We would just ignore them and not even wave. I found out later that Tim was also my father's UPS driver, and he would stop and have prayer with my dad before he would come for lunch. Tim would tell Dad, "Mr. Coker,

Round 2: The Place of My Birth

he hates me!" Then my father would say, "No, it's the Holy Spirit in you that he hates. Tim, you are the only one who can speak to his life, don't stop now." Tim ate lunch at my store for a long time and was faithful to be a light even when I didn't like it.

Tim's son Mike came down to the house to play pool with my boys the afternoon after I had my encounter and deliverance with Jesus. I had found a bottle of alcohol that I had missed the night before and was pouring it out into the sink when he walked in. I told him, "You can take money and buy this stuff, and because you buy it, you think you own it. But if gone unchecked for very long, it will own YOU. Be careful. Jesus came into my life last night and set me free."

Mike ran home and started telling his father, "Dad, something has happened to Mr. Coker."

Tim and I rekindled our friendship. We started walking the neighborhood and praying every night, believing that God was going to answer His promise of healing my marriage. Meanwhile, his wife was glad Susie had left me. Sometimes women don't forgive very fast and they stick together. But it wasn't long before she saw the changes on the inside of me and was won back over to my side. Another lesson was beginning to be learned.

Finding the Place of Blessing

Getting back to my question about Pastor Jimmy. My friend went to the largest Pentecostal church in town, and his pastor—Pastor Jimmy—was one of the ones blocked by God from fathering me. He was the most surprising of all the leaders on the list.

You see, he was the pastor of Central Assembly, a church formed by a split in 1965, back when my father and four uncles were on the board of Treasure Coast Assembly. The board had held one of those votes of confidence, and the current pastor of Treasure left with part of the congregation, despite the board's approval of his leadership. He apparently was a man who took his vision from God, but Central was started out of an act of rebellion. (That's what I've been taught about church splits.) I don't want to throw my father and all my uncles under the bus, but I feel that the cloud of God's favor had moved and, as my father and uncles stayed at Treasure, they missed it. If they had been kingdom thinkers, they would have joined that place of blessing. There is no comparison between the fruitfulness of blessings from Him rather than the approval of a board of men, religious or not.

Look at it this way: If Central closed its doors today, it would be felt all over the city. But if the church that my father had helped to start closed, very few would notice and the city would have no void. Strictly in my own opinion, the effectiveness of the church I was raised in doesn't compare. All the board members are dead except my father, and I can outrun him (maybe?).

With the history of Central stemming from a split, I was hesitant to go there. Sometimes we think our kids don't know what's going on, but kids do pick up offenses that parents have or had. I remember when families left our church and how it was discussed. Yes, it gets into our spirits, and we make judgments in our hearts even when we shouldn't.

Kingdom thinking will help this get routed out of the hearts.

Picking the Right Battles

Since my father was my new spiritual authority, I asked his permission to worship at Central. My friend Tim was very involved there, and it was the happening place. Dad had no problem with me going and was very supportive. He was very pleased that it was a Pentecostal church, and he told me that I didn't have to go to his church but to go were God had sent me.

I went to lunch with the church's pastor (Pastor Jimmy) and told him that I wanted to attend Central and my father had given his approval. He told me it was important to get plugged in with a home group and serve. One great thing was that they had a full-time Christian counselor

Round 2: The Place of My Birth

on staff. That was important because Susie and I were really going to need counseling.

The funny part is, Susie moved back home. I was starting to be the spiritual leader of my home, but she didn't like that church. Firmly, I put my foot down and said, "As the spiritual head of this home, if you're going to live in this house, you will go to church on Sundays." She told me in short order where to go. I pushed the issue, and she said fine. The next Sunday we all got up and headed off to church. But she got into her car and went to a different church. Boy, was I mad! The Lord said, "Pick your battles next time, and be more specific!"

The Lord showed me Ephesians 5:22–25: "Wives, submit to your own husbands, as to the Lord. For the husband is head of the wife, as also Christ is head of the church; and He is the Savior of the body. Therefore, just as the church is subject to Christ, so let the wives be to their own husbands in everything. Husbands, love your wives, just as *Christ also loved the church and gave Himself for her*, that He might sanctify and cleanse her with the washing of water by the word." (emphasis added)

Kingdom Key: Then He said this: "Charlie, until you are willing to die for her, you will always want to kill her."

The church counselor had a few sessions with me and some with Susie. After a few weeks, he got both of us together and said the most shocking thing I have ever heard. This Christian counselor said, "Susie doesn't want to be married to you." He said, "With your history, and, biblically, because of adultery on both sides, God would permit a divorce." He was quoting Mark 10:4 (KJV): "And they said, Moses suffered to write a bill of divorcement, and to put her away. And Jesus answered and said unto them, For the hardness of your heart he wrote you this precept."

Church Fathers vs Kingdom Sons

The church has used the Scriptures to justify divorce, and in many cases it's unavoidable and the right thing to do. But in my case, the King of the kingdom was showing me that if I would let Him take my heart of stone and turn it into a heart of flesh, He would heal my marriage.

The counselor then said, "I don't think your marriage has any hope of making it." But that wasn't up to him to decide. God had made me the promise. No Christian counselor or even my wife can change a promise from God. Take a look at the passage and you will see the reason why the church system has just as high a divorce rate as the world. The hardness of hearts is the root cause of divorce.

The Grace to Grow

Three weeks after I had my encounter with God, I was sitting in church when our town sports hero walked down the aisle and gave his heart back to the Lord. He had played for three championship seasons on the Miami Hurricanes before playing for the New York Jets. While he was down at the altar, I heard the Lord say, "I want you to go welcome your new brother into the kingdom."

I was not going to do that. I said, "Lord, you know that isn't my brother—he's black. A six-foot-four black man who drove a white Lexus and had a white wife. No way on God's green earth was I going to do that! He can't be my brother: he is a n***!" God tried to speak to me about my racism, and I walked out of the church.

The next morning, I got up at 5:30 to read my Bible. When I got right with God, I asked, "How can I know You better?" The Lord said, "By reading My Word." That was a problem because I didn't read well. As I opened the Bible, the first page I turned to was John 14:26: "But the Helper, the Holy Spirit, whom the Father will send in My name, He will teach you all things, and bring to your remembrance all things that I said to you."

I was reading the Bible for the first time in over ten years, and I saw that the Holy Spirit was a teacher. You need to understand … I had a

Round 2: The Place of My Birth

hard time learning to read in school, and I read only on a third-grade level. As I prayed, I asked the Holy Spirit if He would teach me to read. The Lord spoke to me and said if I would give Him one hour in the mornings, He would teach me to read. To make a long story short, He gave me a giant-print King James Bible with no commentary to learn to read. I asked, Why no commentary? He said that He was the author, and He could tell me what the meaning was if I had questions.

As I got up to do my reading the next morning, my King reminded me about my sin problem with black people. Well, I felt His conviction and refused to deal with it. The next morning the same thing. Six days in a row the same conviction. Because of my stubbornness, on the seventh day at 5:30 a.m. I opened my giant-print red-letter Bible and, to my confused little mind, all 1,987 pages of it were blank. Yes, blank: pure white, blank pages, front to back.

I asked the Lord what was going on. He answered me with a stern voice, "Today, you make a choice of keeping your sin of racism or having a relationship with me." I told him that I didn't know how to fix it. He then asked me, "What did you do about your sin three weeks ago, kneeling by your pool table?"

I said, "I confessed it as sin and asked You to forgive me."

"The sin I just showed you in your heart this morning can be washed white as snow with the same prayer."

I asked the Lord to forgive me of the sin of racism. I spoke quietly, "I don't know how it got there, but if it doesn't please You, take it away."

Then the Lord asked me to start praying every day for this couple. My first prayer may not be exciting to you, but it was to God that day; He knows my heart. It went like this: "Dear Jesus, bless that n*** and his white wife. Please help then to walk with You." Old habits take time to change, and the Lord was gracious with me. In the kingdom, there is always grace to grow. The writing returned to the pages of my Bible, and the King of my heart was very pleased with me.

Church Fathers vs Kingdom Sons

As I look back, my stay at Central was very short, but I was exposed to a lot of what I walk in ministry today. The apostolic, the prophetic, and my true passion—healing the body of Christ of racism—are what this church exposed me to. Pastor Jimmy was very loving and helpful. But it became apparent that God had a different fellowship for my family. He blessed me when I told him that God was moving my family to a Baptist church in town. It was my decision to leave.

As I look back I see that while God put me in Central for only about six weeks, much happened in that short time. This was the first time I had been exposed to the prophetic, and this pastor is an apostle.

Back in 1993, the apostolic was just starting to be released into the body of Christ. It has been great reflecting back and seeing the different anointing and callings working according to Ephesians 4:11–13: "And He Himself gave some to be apostles, some prophets, some evangelists, and some pastors and teachers, for the equipping of the saints for the work of ministry, for the edifying of the body of Christ, till we all come to the unity of the faith and of the knowledge of the Son of God, to a perfect man, to the measure of the stature of the fullness of Christ."

This very short time was very enlightening, showing my calling and my personal inheritance from God. I didn't know then what God was doing, but He was starting to train me to see the kingdom and rule with kingdom principles, all the while submitting to the church systems.

***

Kingdom Keys:

1. Holy fear of the King and His kingdom is helpful for gaining wisdom and understanding.
2. The King can set you free from whatever has you in bondage.
3. Kingdom thinking will unite and not divide.

Round 2: The Place of My Birth

4. Kingdom is a generational view of where we came from and where we are going.
5. Kingdom principles don't work well with a hard heart.
6. The King of the kingdom will not tolerate racism.
7. Until you're willing to die for your spouse, you will want to kill them.

Round 3

Living for Jesus, Baptist Style

As the Lord started moving on my heart to look for a different church, I was becoming irritated in my spirit and could not figure it out.

The kingdom works within a smaller gate of tolerance when it comes to relationships. If you have an issue with your brother, go make it right. The kingdom lifestyle that Jesus was teaching me was a lifestyle of repentance. He gave me a teaching one day about false accusations. He asked how badly I wanted to be like Him. I said that I was willing to change as fast as I could to His image. Then He gave me a principle to live by.

"Charlie, there is always enough truth in every false accusation that you can repent and become more like Me, improve and become more like Me, either in flesh or spirit."

Well, the Lord told me to go see Tommy, an old friend of mine. We had had grown up together, and I was to let him know that I had given my heart over to the Lord. Tommy had gotten saved and was a deacon in a Baptist church in Winter Beach, Florida. The year before, we had gone hunting in Missouri. He had started to witness to me like my friend Tim had, but I was in no frame of mind to hear about God and I had a rifle in my hand.

I knocked, and Tommy came to the door. He had a look of surprise, but as I told him about my conversion he started to tear up. He said, "Last week the Lord told me to give you a call, but I didn't."

"So why didn't you?"

He spoke further. "Last time I tried to tell you about Jesus, you threatened to shoot me. Remember?"

"I got saved," I retorted.

As we talked, Tommy started telling me about a course for new believers at the Baptist church called "Survival Kit." As he continued, I was feeling like the Lord was telling me to commit to the course. At first, I would not do it because I am Pentecostal, and we don't believe the same way as Baptists do. I gave in and told Tommy I would pray about it.

"I will pray about it" has become a standard answer among Christians who actually want to say, "Heck no! I am not going to do that." But I knew it was my King telling me to commit. I had dealt with many things in my life during the prior few weeks and was in NO mood to deal with religious Baptists who believed that "once saved, always saved"; don't believe in divine healing; and don't speak in tongues. No way was I going to let a religious spirit stop my progress in coming to spiritual maturity!

Following the Path of Peace

About a week later, Tommy's sister, a friend of Susie's, came by the house to pick something up. She had heard that I had become a Christian and was happy for me. She stated, "You know, Charlie, I am taking a course for new believers at my brother's church called 'Survival Kit.' You should come and learn how to survive this new life in Christ."

I did it again: "Leeann, I will 'pray about it.'" As she left, I felt like I had grieved the Holy Spirit, but I was not going to talk about it. I was not going to go to a Baptist church!

I was becoming very agitated in my spirit and understood why. This is what grieving the Spirit feels like. My new King was not pleased with

Round 3: Living for Jesus, Baptist Style

me, and my peace was gone. My King is also the Prince of Peace, so if my peace had left, I was not right.

Kingdom Key: If your peace has left, you're not right!

The "Ticket" to Survival

About a week later, I was miserable inside. I had to go to one of my rental houses to try to fix the pool pump, as some glass had lodged in the screen. While I was trying to fix it, I cut my finger and it started to bleed. That was it! I started praying and asking God to help me. I was trying to live for Him, but I was miserable and hurting. My wife was hostile and trying to move on, and she didn't want our marriage to work.

I started driving home, and as I was going down Twentieth Avenue, a state trooper pulled me over and asked for my license and registration. As he started to write me a ticket for speeding, I began to weep. This new King wanted to talk about the prayer that I had prayed a few minutes ago. Well, the trooper looked at me and asked if I was okay. The more he wrote, the more I cried. I was really crying hard and couldn't stop. The trooper asked again, "Mr. Coker, are you okay? What's the problem? It's only a speeding ticket."

And then, because I felt this would stop him from asking me any more questions, I blurted out, "I am a new Christian, and I thought things would be better if I gave my heart to Jesus. I am miserable; just give me my ticket so I can go home." The trooper put his ticket book down on the front seat and said, "Mr. Coker, I know this Jesus you gave your heart to pretty well." For over forty-five minutes, sitting beside the road, he prayed for the situation with my family and blessed me.

Continuing on, he spoke gently. "Mr. Coker, since you're a new Christian, we have this course at my Baptist church called 'Survival

Church Fathers vs Kingdom Sons

Kit.' Would you like to come and learn how to survive?" God set me up, and I said, "Yes, I sure do. I don't need to pray about this one any longer." I figured with all that prayer I was off the hook, but no, he still gave me a $158 ticket ... "Obedience is better than sacrifice."

So I went to meet the pastor, Lou, of this Baptist church; I had a few issues to overcome about Baptists and what I had been taught over my lifetime.

At our meeting, he was very gracious. As I started to tell him my prejudiced beliefs about Baptists, I exposed my ungodly judgments. As he spoke, the King living inside of me helped me to understand that there was church doctrine that was given authority by the leaders, and then there are kingdom principles. They are not the same. That reality hit me like a ton of bricks!

Pastor Lou** reviewed my dislikes and started addressing them one by one:

"So you think we don't believe in speaking in tongues? Let's look at Acts 2." He showed me in Scripture and explained it. His answer surprised me. He said that he believed it is a gift from God, but it has been misused and that if I had the gift, he was all right with it.

What about divine healing? He wondered aloud if I was sick. I said, "No, I wasn't."

"Then what's the problem? We do believe in divine healing." He then read me the Scripture where the elders are to be called and anoint the sick with oil. "What other questions can I help you with?"

Pastor Lou said Baptists believe that once saved, always saved, and asked me if I was saved. I said, "Yes, of course."

Then he asked, "Are you going to stay saved?" I replied, "Of course."

"Then what's the problem?" He hugged me and welcomed me to the family. I started "Survival Kit" the following Thursday night.

Round 3: Living for Jesus, Baptist Style

The Lord spoke to me about corporate authority. He let me know firmly that if I exercised my gifts and offended the authority to which I was submitted, that I would surely be in rebellion and would suffer the consequences.

He showed me how to release the kingdom without speaking in Pentecostal language. I learned to heal in Jesus's name without screaming. I learned to give prophecy in parables. I studied and became an instructor for several Bible study courses, including: "Survival Kit," "Experiencing God," "Search for Significance," and "Prayer Time."

I learned so much from this fellowship. There was a deacon whose sons weren't going to church. I used to hunt and fish with them. He asked me to do what my dad did with Tim. I was to witness to them, so they'd return to church. I finally made him aware that the boys knew all the sin, gossip, and backbiting that the pastors and leaders were involved in. Therefore, they weren't interested in his Jesus, and I was powerless to be a witness. The kingdom mouth speaks.

> Finally, brethren, whatsoever things are true, whatsoever things are honest, whatsoever things are just, whatsoever things are pure, whatsoever things are lovely, whatsoever things are of good report; if there be any virtue, and if there be any praise, think on these things. Those things, which ye have both learned, and received, and heard, and seen in me, do: and the God of peace shall be with you (Philippians 4:8–9 KJV).

When God showed me in Houston that Pastor Lou was one whose heart He had hardened and would not allow to father me, I felt sorry. But now I know why. He had a moral failure that had destroyed many lives. This was heartbreaking to watch! I do know that he did get some healing for himself and his family, and they are doing well.

Church Fathers vs Kingdom Sons

If I had not gone to this Baptist church, I would not be as foundationally solid with my Bible as I am now and would not have the heart to disciple people like I do.

Taking Authority over Fear

The Christmas of 1993 was a good, but hard, time for me. Susie said that she was going to move back home for Christmas, but only for the boys. After Christmas, she was out of there.

One night in prayer the Lord spoke to me quietly, to my heart, in the still, small voice. But it thundered in my head. "She will not leave again. Stop walking in fear."

> For the thing I greatly feared has come upon me, and
> what I dreaded has happened to me (Job 3:25).

The Lord was trying to bring deliverance from the spirit of fear in my life. Job 3:25 also deals with the things you dread: When you give place to fear, you will have a spirit of dread also. When Susie would tell me that she was going to leave, I would crumble in fear. But after the Lord set me free, I was willing to serve God with or without her. So one day she got mad and told me that if I didn't do what she wanted she was leaving.

I boldly told her that I was the spiritual authority in this house. If she had a problem with that, then "don't let the door hit you where the good Lord split you." But I was the authority, and the fear of her leaving was broken that day.

I have seen fear of a spouse leaving steal the true destiny of many who have high callings on their lives.

On February 14, 1994—Valentine's Day—we went to the church my mother and dad had attended for forty-five years. Susie and I looked and saw twenty couples at the altar renewing their marriage vows. Susie said she only did it to get me off her back. But it was just like the vision,

Round 3: Living for Jesus, Baptist Style

and we renewed our marriage vows. From that day forward, we haven't used the word "divorce." (We have used "murder," but not "divorce.")

My business partner was also someone I feared. He was starting to become very displeased with my relationship with my newfound King because I had begun to bring some changes to the company.

Perfect Will or Permissive Will

Jesus started dealing with me about some of the business practices we were doing, like taking cash and not reporting it. (I sure do miss that!) I really didn't want to deal with him on this matter because I had started to make so many changes and this was sacred cash.

After I argued with God for several weeks, He finally asked me if I was willing to confront the issue, if that were His requirement. He reminded me of Job 3:25. I had given fear time to turn to dread. When God broke through, asking if I was willing to confront, I told Him yes. Peace came, and He said, "Great—I will handle that for you, since you have now become willing." The burden to confront the issue was released.

About two weeks later, my business partner came running into the office. He was angry and scared. He started yelling: "Your blankety-blank wife is going to ruin us. I ran into her at the 7-Eleven today, and she still is going to divorce you. She said all she wants out of this marriage is what's fair, and she knows about the cash we take." He started telling me that we had to stop doing that and start running every dime through the books properly.

Kingdom Key: Unbridled fear will turn into dread. Dread will develop into depression, and depression will kill your dreams and destiny.

Church Fathers vs Kingdom Sons

It amazes me how God used a spirit of fear to His advantage when I needed Him to. All I had to be was willing.

Shortly thereafter, he told me that there was not enough room in the company for me with Jesus. It felt as if he were forcing me to choose—I had to get rid of Jesus if I wanted to stay, or both of us needed to get out. I knew that this partnership was going to be short-lived. God started showing me it was time to make a choice.

I began to have angelic encounters and was being shown my inheritance of the kingdom, which was in Vero Beach, Florida. God showed me the principalities over the region and city, and how to defeat them in some areas. The realm of the Spirit was coming alive!

The Lord sent a business for me to buy in Orange City, Florida. It was a lighting store that a former youth pastor who lived in Vero had started, so I started praying about moving.

One night the Lord gave me two choices: His perfect will or His permissive will for my life. He said that He would bless either one.

First, He showed me that if I chose to stay in Vero, He would remove my business partner and prosper me financially, more than I had dreamed. But if I stayed in Vero, He could not promise me my family.

Second, if I moved, He wanted to use me in ministry. He would never leave me or forsake me, but it would not be easy. However, my family would be restored and He would be with me.

I knew it would be a no-brainer for most, but Susie was still hurting and angry, and she didn't want to be married. My kids weren't real happy about life with a spiritual father who had changed before their eyes either.

Money or family—which do I chose?

I told God I was all in. Let Your perfect will be done in my life.

Round 3: Living for Jesus, Baptist Style

The King living on the inside of me let me know He had a plan that was not only sufficient, but satisfying, if only I would follow Him: a ministry that would take me around the world!

Susie and I came into agreement and we moved to Deltona, Florida.

As I look back, I am grateful that the Holy Spirit trained me so fast. What I was about to walk into would have killed me had I not listened and learned about the kingdom. I remember when the Holy Spirit spoke to me one night and said, "Charlie, I can do more in six months with a man who will obey than I can with some in sixty years. How badly do you want to mature?"

I said, "Give me the fast track. I can handle it."

So the Lord told me to cross out Scripture and rewrite it: in 1 Samuel 15:22, the Lord had me cross out "to obey is better than sacrifice" and change it to read, "Charlie, obey or you will become the sacrifice."

That's the fast-track kingdom training course!

***

Kingdom Keys:

1. The kingdom incorporates all of those who have received the King. ALL. Therefore, preferences are allowed, but not prejudice.
2. The kingdom has a language of its own: True, Noble, Just, Pure, Lovely, Kind, and of Good Report.
3. Kingdom principle of business: Don't be unequally yoked.
4. Kingdom fast-track training course: Obedience.
5. If your peace has left, you're not right!
6. Unbridled fear will turn into dread, dread will develop into depression, and depression will kill your dreams and destiny.

Round 4

Leave Your Father's House

> Now the Lord had said to Abram: "Get out of your country, from your family and from your father's house, to a land that I will show you" (Genesis 12:1).

Personally, I love this passage of Scripture. Then read verses 2 and 3: "I will make you a great nation; I will bless you and make your name great; and you shall be a blessing. I will bless those who bless you, and I will curse him who curses you; and in all of the families of the earth shall be blessed."

This passage has taught me so much, because God told Abraham to leave his father's house and his family. This was a personal prophecy from God to Abraham. I want you to pay attention to verse 4: "And Lot went with him." It's interesting to note that because of Abraham's disobedience, he failed to have another personal prophecy directed to him until after Lot and Abraham separated: "Then Lot chose for himself all the plain of Jordan, and Lot journeyed east. And they separated from each other" (Gen. 13:11).

The personal words from God about Abraham's destiny did not come till after Lot and he had separated.

Look at verses 14 to 18:

> And the Lord said to Abram, after Lot had separated from him: "Lift your eyes *now* and look from the place

where you are—northward, southward, eastward, and westward; for all the land, which you see I give to you and your descendants forever. And I will make your descendants as the dust of the earth; so that if a man could number the dust of the earth, then your descendants also could be numbered. Arise, walk in the land through its length and its width, for I give it to you." Then Abram moved his tent, and went and dwelt by the terebinth trees of Mamre, which are in Hebron, and built an altar there to the Lord. (emphasis added)

This passage of Scripture has been instrumental for my understanding, because I see that Abraham is a great man of faith in Scripture. As I study his life, I see the process God took him through to make him the man of faith. From my viewpoint, Abraham acted a lot like a spiritual orphan; like me, always afraid to stand alone. I recognize this as the mindset of a spiritual orphan. It has taken me years to dismantle that way of thinking and feeling and replace it properly with the understanding of Sonship.

Moving away from Vero Beach, where my family roots ran back five generations, was very difficult to do. But the Lord showed me that it was vital for me to deal with some areas in my family and that if I didn't relocate, He would not be able to heal us and make us a family.

Learning the Faithfulness of God

We made the decision to purchase the lighting store in Orange City. The first day in Deltona, after my father drove the moving truck back to Vero Beach, we loaded up in my SUV and went to get some pizza. As we drove out of the driveway of the small three-bedroom, two-bath house we had rented in a section of town that my family was not used to living in, my oldest son, Jason, said the most hurtful thing I had ever heard, "Dad, look at the car we are driving. This thing has 120,000 miles on it, and it's the best vehicle we have. Did you see the house you moved us into? Dad, you're turning us into "dirtballs."

Round 4: Leave Your Father's House

Man … that statement hurt me to the core. The next morning, I went to the Lord about that statement and why it hurt so much. The Lord showed me that I had always given my family nice homes in great neighborhoods and had been a good provider, but I had been their source and not Him. The Lord asked if I really wanted Him to answer the prayers I had been praying for my family. He showed me in a vision how He was going to strip me of my ability to provide for my family financially as I had before. He said, "When you allow Me to remove your ability to provide as in the past and teach your family how to rely on God, then I will be able to cultivate godly relationships with your family."

He told me that He would also take care of us as we learned about His faithfulness. It was so hard to have foreknowledge that the Lord was removing the grace I had walked in, as a backslidden Christian, to make money! This was the hardest season in business I ever had. For years, I had been able to make money in the lighting business, but I had always had a partner who would help me. I was a natural salesman. Now, for the first time in business, I had to work on my weaknesses, which seemed to parallel my spiritual life.

The truth be known, I was a very poor businessman. I had great people skills, but I don't feel like I was a true entrepreneur. I strove harder and longer to overcompensate. I had always been a workaholic and was driven by fear of failure. I have come to the revelation that this is one of the main character traits of a spiritual orphan.

I was beginning to realize that I truly desired to be in full-time ministry and that God was using my business as a training tool to show me how the kingdom works and to mold me into His image.

Building relationships from scratch in a new town was very difficult. Being away from family and friends, learning to walk with Jesus, and learning how to fit within a megachurch was a little overwhelming to say the least! Within a few weeks, the Lord spoke to me about becoming a member of a Trinity Assembly of God church with over 1,500 members and a private school for my boys to attend. The instruction from the

Church Fathers vs Kingdom Sons

Lord was very clear and precise: "I am sending you to a church to serve Me under a man who is My servant. But if you get your eyes off of Me, the snakes in this place will bite you and take you out! This is your test to pass or fail!"

It was a very basic, clear instruction with a test at the end. As I looked at this, I saw that God was sending me to a church, not a man. He was God's servant, but there was never a promise to be mentored or fathered. "Lord, what are you doing to me?" I cried out. "I have this kingdom view of the King and His kingdom, and You are sending me into an old wineskin."

I want to be very careful not to be disrespectful or dishonoring to the Lord or to His servant, but this was the biggest test and training for kingdom living. You may ask why everything I learn has to be a kingdom view. If the kingdom is anything, then it is everything.

Authority and Honor

The first Sunday that my wife and family went to Trinity, I walked down the aisle and shook the hand of Pastor Raymond**. I told him that the Lord was sending us to serve him at the church and asked if we could have an appointment or do lunch some time. Shockingly, he admitted that he was pretty busy and that that would probably never happen. As I was shaking his hand, I went into a vision and the Lord showed me those snakes He told me about. I began a three-day prayer meeting to make sure I had heard God, and I tried to renegotiate my position of obedience.

The Lord started to teach me about authority and honor at a kingdom level in ways I had never experienced before. He gave me Psalm 105:15, saying, "Do not touch My anointed ones, and do My prophets no harm." The Lord spoke this to me one day: "You can't have what you don't honor." He said that I was "learning to do war with honor with my father, and the principles don't change even when the realm of authority does."

Round 4: Leave Your Father's House

When God has shown you the snake side of a ministry and then tells you to never speak evil about a pastor and to protect him from his enemies, you learn that kingdom culture always looks for God and the goodness of God in every relationship and situation. "People see what they are looking for." God was teaching me to look to Him in all things.

> **Kingdom culture always looks for God and the goodness of God in every relationship and situation.**

Pastor Raymond was (and still is) the best preacher that I have ever been in ministry with, by far. He would preach with wisdom and power, and people would get saved every Sunday. There I would sit in amazement at what God showed me, and then see the mantle of ministry cover him like a blanket and the power of God manifest. Soon I learned that God had his hand on his life: you don't start with twenty-seven people and grow to a 1,500 to 2,000-member church without God's calling on your life.

He was a professional CEO preacher and carried a spirit of excellence at a level I had never experienced before—a strong leader who left no room for misbehaving.

I learned about positional authority by watching how the mantle of ministry on Pastor Raymond worked as he stood in his office and preached. Notice in John 11:51, the Word says: "Now this he did not say on his own authority; but being high priest that year he prophesied that Jesus would die for the nation." After study of this particular Scripture, I came to understand that there is authority and anointing due to the position. I call this "positional authority." What I've come to realize is that many of the people in church look for positional authority and avoid the protocol of the kingdom, which is only attained by pursuing a relationship with the Holy Spirit.

Church Fathers vs Kingdom Sons

I was getting restless, eager to do some teaching or preaching, when one of the associate pastors told me that no one teaches at Trinity until they had been proven faithful for at least two years with no problems. That rule ticked me off, and I had it out for this guy. Very abruptly I told him that God didn't send me there to sit on some stinking pew and rot, and I would do what God sent me there to do. I had been teaching "Survival Kit" to new believers in Vero Beach before I came to Deltona. When I asked how I could use the training I had, I was advised that it was a Baptist course and basically told to sit down and do what I was told.

> **Many of the people in church look for positional authority and avoid the protocol of the kingdom, which is only attained by pursuing a relationship with the Holy Spirit.**

At this point, I was beginning to become labeled as a man in rebellion. The day the associate pastor called me a wild stallion, I looked at him and snapped back, "At least I still have the equipment to reproduce and am not a gelding like you." Believe it or not, the next book that I am writing is *How to Win Friends*.

Acting Like a Child of God

I started telling God He had better do something, or I was going to have a hissy fit. Look, the Bible tells us to come to God like a child. Once in a great while, a hissy fit would work with my dad, but only if the reason was a noble one. If it were manipulating or doing stupid stuff, he would not tolerate it whatsoever.

People often tell me that I talk to God with disrespect and that they would be afraid to act that way. The difference is that I know when He is on His throne ruling as God and when we are in the garden and He is

Round 4: Leave Your Father's House

Father. When He is in the garden, I can tell Him how I feel about where He has me and how some of His other children are frustrating me and exposing some anger or fear where I need some help. Papa God has always been concerned about me, and sometimes that's what it takes to move His hand in my favor.

I remember Papa God taking me to the woodshed and punishing me one day, and while I was crying, I sat down by the lake. He came and sat next to me and started telling me how much of a pleasure it was disciplining me. I said, "PLEASURE?! You have to be kidding me. You thought that was fun?"

God replied, "I didn't say 'fun'! I said 'pleasure.'"

"Explain, please."

He said, "It's not very often that I get the pleasure of disciplining one of My sons because he's trying too hard to please Me." Continuing further, He counseled, "This is the kind of disciplining that will train a teachable Son to rule the kingdom in righteousness."

So there are times you have to find Papa God in the garden and throw a hissy fit. A hissy fit with wrong motives will get you a lot of trouble. Your motives have to be pure.

The revelation that I was receiving about the kingdom was starting to take root deep in my heart. All the while, I was witnessing a ministry at extreme levels of anointing and fruitfulness, yet I was experiencing a revelation of a hidden snake side.

One day, while I was in church listening to this great preacher preach, I heard the Lord say, "I'm trying to bring you to a new level of maturity."

I asked, "Lord, what does maturity look like?"

He answered, "Maturity is being able to discern the truth even when it's spoken from a liar."

Church Fathers vs Kingdom Sons

I watched, listened, and learned, and I found that the gifts and calling of God are without repentance.

During this season of our life, my wife and I were learning to communicate better and attempting to raise our children in a kingdom culture.

The results of me throwing a hissy fit to God were this: I had gone with our music minister one Saturday night to Tampa. As we drove, I shared my testimony on how God had visited me personally and started healing my marriage and how I had been taken advantage of financially by an old business partner.

Freedom to Teach

The next morning at church, a guest speaker got up to speak the message. He started releasing a vision he had had the night before. There I was, sitting in the back of a very large church, and this man was starting to prophesy about a businessman who had been taken advantage of financially and God had sent him to this church to teach Bible courses to new believers. He was prophesying my life! I wanted to escape by hiding under the pew, but the music minister looked right at me and said, "Charlie, he is talking about you."

The preacher publicly started, saying, "Sir, come here, I need to lay my hands on you." He prophesied my life story, how I had been sent to that city and to that church to raise up new believers. As he laid hands on me, I was slain in the spirit and I landed at the feet of Pastor Raymond.

Once I got up off the floor and sat down, I said to the Holy Spirit, "There is nothing he prophesied that You have not already told me personally." Then the Lord told me, "That word was not for you; it was for Pastor."

The following day, Pastor Raymond called me into his office. He said that obviously I had clout with God and released me to teach "Survival Kit"

Round 4: Leave Your Father's House

to new believers. When I started my new believer's class, called "Survival Kit," they felt it was not going to be successful because it was a Baptist course. The Lord proved Himself faithful, and attendance doubled every class.

The lessons I learned were more about segregation versus congregation or church versus kingdom. When leadership segregates, they can control and have hidden areas in their lives. Leadership becomes hierarchal and less relational. Many of the leaders with whom I am in ministry today have come from this ministry and found God to be faithful.

I discovered later that one of the board members, who is a private investigator by trade, had investigated me to try to dig up some dirt on me. I asked what his report back to the pastor was. His report was that I was an open book and brutally honest and there was nothing that was hidden in any way. One of the kingdom principles God taught me a long time ago was, "If you can't talk about your past, you're probably still connected to it, or it still has influence in your life."

Trinity had become our family. My wife and I sang in the choir, which was over 150 strong, and the power of God would show up every Sunday. I was teaching "Survival Kit" and had started a men's group. I was flourishing in ministry, and my spiritual gifting was starting to emerge with great accuracy. There was a group of newly married men working together with older men. We got on fire and were starting to become a force to be reckoned with.

If you can't talk about your past, you're probably still connected to it, or it still has influence in your life.

Although this church family had become our life, in the back of my mind I could still see the things that God had shown me. And we could sense that something was going on behind the scenes. Several of the founding members who had been pillars of the church spiritually and financially were starting to be ousted. There were starting to be public displays of open rebukes coming from board members and outside ministries during services. There was a local church that started picketing outside the building with signs, trying to expose the sins of the church.

Serious Warnings

One night, I had this warning dream for one of the men who served on the board. I visited his home and spoke to him along with his wife with a warning from the Lord: "Touch not Mine anointed and do My prophets no harm." It's hard to tell a businessman to be careful when he approaches a leader. Even when you're right, there should be proper protocol based on respect and rank.

Senior leaders are ultimately responsible to God and then to the leadership around them. There are definitely defined lines of authority; many times, it's only by the discernment of spirits we can know where one line of authority starts and the other ends. There may come a point when leadership will not listen to the Holy Spirit or anyone else who has been put in a position to hold us accountable to our calling and integrity. That's when you have to completely trust God.

> **When God judges with mercy, its purpose is always to draw us back to Him.**

On October 16, 1996, a very clear and prophetic dream showed me that it was time to leave Trinity: and that's when we left. I was accused of being in rebellion and that I would not submit to authority. The dream also gave me an indication that there was going to be judgment released against the church. Not only judgments of wrath, but also judgments of mercy. When God judges with mercy, its purpose is always to draw us back to Him.

Round 4: Leave Your Father's House

Surrounded by the Presence of God

The following day, I was at a Promise Keepers meeting in Jacksonville, Florida, with 30,000 to 40,000 men praising God. I looked over my right shoulder and I saw the glory cloud of God coming over the top of the stadium. As I watched, the cloud began to settle upon me and God started speaking to me, spirit to Spirit; His holiness was so intense I felt like I was breathing liquid love and I was going to die.

Embraced fully in the Father's love, the Lord started showing me how He wanted me to leave Trinity for a short season. I was to go to a smaller church, where the minister would receive me, and he would give me time to preach in his pulpit. In this particular encounter, the Lord showed me my calling and how He was going to use me to awaken America in areas of racism and religious tradition. As the glory descended upon me, there was a fifty-yard radius in which everyone around me laid out under the power of God.

He spoke, and I started debating with Him about my oldest son, Jason, and about how my marriage was barely livable, and the Lord was telling me to preach the gospel. I started quoting Scriptures back to God: "For if a man does not know how to rule his own house, how will he take care of the church of God?" (1 Timothy 3:5). My son Jason was still battling drugs, and there's no way I could have stood in the pulpit and preached the truth. At that moment, the Lord told me to preach in faith what He had promised me about my family. He said, "I will heal your son and I will finish healing your marriage as you preach My Word." While I was in the glory, God continued, "I am putting a mantle of My glory on you to do the work of the ministry. Charlie, continue to pursue the anointing (in you) for relationship and direction, so that the anointing that is (on you) will do the work of the ministry."

On the trip home from this Promise Keepers meeting, I laid my head on the passenger side door and wept most of the way. I pleaded with the Lord, asking what He meant by "the anointing in me giving direction, so that the anointing on me would do the work." The Lord spoke instead, "I will bless whom you tell Me to bless." As I was lying there in the dark, talking to the Holy Spirit, I said, "Holy Spirit, bless Steve." Suddenly, Steve (who was driving) was almost wiped out in the Spirit and started yelling, "Stop that!"

I responded, "What? I didn't do anything." So instead, I said, "Holy Spirit, bless the guys in the back seat": and whoosh—the Holy Spirit manifested great power, and they were laid out under it.

The following week, I had an appointment with Pastor and told him that I was leaving. Sure enough, just as the dream had showed, I was labeled rebellious and unwilling to submit to authority. It's amazing how God can show you something and let you know it's coming, but once it comes, we still have to choose to operate in the flesh or walk in the Spirit.

The following week I went to a pastor in the town next to us, Orange City. As I walked to his office, I told the pastor, "God has told me to come to your church." As I revealed to him that God had sent me to him, he opened his calendar and started picking dates on which he was going to let me preach. The Lord had spoken to him and told him that I was coming: "God said a man was going to come and I was to give him my pulpit so that he could be training for the ministry." The Lord told him that the sins of another man had kept me out of the pulpit. God told him I would be in his church for a season, and to give me as much pulpit time as he could.

It amazes me how Christians can get caught up in gossip and slander, just as the dream had warned me. I was going to be labeled rebellious and unwilling to submit to authority. I was called a wild stallion. All the while, I started preaching and using my gifts to expand the kingdom.

Revealing the Skeletons

Several months later, a local news station videotaped my old pastor at a topless bar dipping dollars. This particular scandal was shocking, to say the least. It brought division among family members, among church

Round 4: Leave Your Father's House

members, and to a city and region, and the devil had a heyday. At first he denied it was he; claiming it was someone else. It was fascinating to see the things I learned as I watched how a large denomination handles situations like this. Needless to say, the body of Christ was coming apart. My wife and I were still amazed, even after I had the prophetic insights that I had, and we did doubt in our minds if this could actually be true. How does a man with this much anointing, with this much power from God, get videotaped in that situation? (There but for the grace of God go I.)

As the exposure of corruption became obvious, the skeletons that people had kept locked in their closets started coming out in all kinds of accusations. There was talk about sexual abuse many years before. Some said that he was a drug dealer; others rumored that he took all of the board members to the topless bars in Orlando. Some of the rumors claimed to be backed up, and many were being played on national television. The district officials were very slow in their response. That alone left room for the enemy to destroy many people's lives and their ability to trust in the Lord Jesus or His church. But the Lord was always telling me to "touch not His anointed and do His prophets no harm."

The rumor mill gushed like a raging river and revealed more skeletons, and more accusations were sent swirling through the news media, both local and national. All the while, the body of Christ was searching for the truth, in many cases unwilling to face the truth that this could actually be happening.

Several months before I had left the church, my wife and I had met with Pastor about my calling into the ministry. I struggled with business, since I wanted to be in the ministry. Pastor tried to convince me that I should definitely stay in business and not the ministry. We had a discussion in which I told him I wanted to preach in his pulpit, and in no uncertain terms he pretty well told me it would never happen. The problem was, the Lord had showed me that I was going to speak behind that pulpit, and he informed me, "over his dead body." Without hesitation, I boldly stated, "You know, I believe God can arrange that."

Church Fathers vs Kingdom Sons

The first part of the year after the videotape had been exposed, I had a prophetic encounter that gave me a message from the book of Esther where the Jews had a legal right to destroy all of their enemies, but God told them not to. That night I called the leader who was in charge of the church at the time and explained the word the Lord had given me. He released me to minister. So, the pulpit that the pastor said I would never preach behind was now available for me to release the word of the Lord.

That night I preached, prophesied, and made some bold statements about how God would use a Hittite or Jebusite to bring judgment upon His children. Such a person would bring forth spiritual judgment and correction and would bless him and release him, and that He would bring in a Hittite or Jebusite to execute a judgment of mercy. Biblically, we are supposed to judge ourselves lest we be judged, but in this situation the Lord said release and He would bring in a non-Israelite.

I was told by one of the board members later that night that they were making a decision on whether to press criminal charges. They decided to obey the word of the Lord, brought proper correction to the best of their ability, blessed, and released.

Two weeks later, because of the videotape being released publicly by the news organizations, the state of Florida filed charges and charged the pastor with drug trafficking, kidnapping, and pistol-whipping a man over drugs. The accusations were atrocious. All I knew is that he had plea bargained for a lesser sentence.

Praying for Restoration

Several months later, the Lord gave me a prophetic dream. When I woke up, I read the story of how Samson had lost his strength by the cutting of his hair. I realized that after his hair was restored, the Lord used him one more time. He pulled down the two pillars, and at the end of his life, after his hair had grown back, he killed more of the enemy in his final move than he had previously in his entire ministry.

Round 4: Leave Your Father's House

As I read this story, the Lord spoke to me about my pastor. He said, "When his hair grows back, the end of his ministry will be greater than the beginning." Of course, the Lord asked me if I would be willing to restore him back to the pulpit. I replied, "I don't even like this man," and it was evident that he didn't like me. But the Lord showed me how much I had learned to love him, honor him, and respect him because of the calling and the mantle that was on his life. I told the Lord if that was what He wanted me to do, I would do it.

As my wife got up that morning, I shared the encounter I'd had with God about Pastor. I told her that the Lord had said, "When his hair grows back, his ministry will be greater in the end than the beginning." That morning, as I opened the newspaper to read while eating my breakfast, I saw a picture of my pastor with his head shaved, as he had been sentenced to prison.

At that moment I came to the conclusion that my choices had better be righteous in God's eyes. I started counteracting in prayer all the word curses from the church leaders in our community. I came into more resistance from Christian leaders than from the world. I was certain that the enemy would have a field day with Pastor's life and anyone who chose to stand beside him.

One sign that the Lord had given me was to ask me if I were willing to restore someone that I did not agree with, did not like, and didn't trust. Pastor didn't like me or trust me, either. But God always has a plan ...

I knew that the calling for ministry was on my life. I told God that I had made the choice for His perfect will, and anything less would not be tolerated. I took a day off and spent it with God, seeking His wisdom to be sure that I would never become a public disgrace to the ministry or Him. I made a covenant with God, giving Him permission to kill me and take me off the face of the earth before I created a scandal that became a reproach to His name. Several people feel that I speak about God killing me too much, but it sure does curb one's appetite for sin.

Church Fathers vs Kingdom Sons

***

Kingdom Keys:

1. Maturity is being able to discern the truth, even when it's spoken from a liar.
2. If you can't talk about your past, you're probably still connected to it, or it still has influence in your life.
3. When your history disrupts your present, it will hinder your future. So make your history His story.

Round 5

Surviving the Snakes of Church

Not Becoming a Snake Yourself

This is one of the hardest lessons I've ever had to learn. Because of my gifting and personality, I have a tendency to be extremely critical. However, the Holy Spirit has taught me that critical behavior is highly unacceptable for walking in kingdom principles.

One day, I was sitting in church listening to the preacher preach, and I was both critical and judgmental of his delivery style and his insight into Scripture. The Lord rebuked me sharply: "Are you ever going to mature, so I can put you in a position of authority and use you to properly judge My house, or are you always going to sit in the seat of the scornful?"

God told me that He would never use me to bring revelation of judgment unless I was willing to walk the person through the healing process while restoring them back to wholeness.

> **Kingdom Key: God will never release you to pronounce judgment unless you're willing to walk with the person to bring healing and wholeness if there is repentance.**

That's one standard that will make you count the cost before you speak!

Church Fathers vs Kingdom Sons

I knew the Lord was quoting Psalm 1:1: "Blessed is the man who walks not in the counsel of the ungodly nor stands in the path of sinners nor sits in the seat of the scornful." The Lord took me in a vision and showed me the throne that He had prepared for me to rule from. It was a very high-backed chair. As I sat on this throne, there was a plaque over my head that first read "Son," then changed to "Priest," and changed again to "King."

I saw these three plaques above my head, and the Lord spoke to me about the positions of authority He was trying to give me. "Rather than using the throne as a source of praise and encouragement, your seat became a source of scorn. THAT'S a problem." A plaque that had "Scornful" written on it rose above my head. The Lord reminded me that I have authority and that He was giving me a place of honor in which to sit.

As the Lord started to chastise me about my attitude, my criticisms, and my false judgments, and how they were the reason that I had turned my place of authority into the seat of the scornful, my eyes started tearing up and I began to weep. HOW could I stop being so critical and judgmental, since it had become second nature to me? I prayed for the Lord to help me so that I could sit in my seat of authority, judge in righteousness, and make a difference in the earthly realm.

The Lord began explaining to me that He would teach me how to sit in a place of authority, and that I would no longer turn that place of authority into the seat of the scornful, but I would judge properly. As I pleaded with the Lord to please help me, He turned my seat upside down and started driving three long nails through the bottom of the seat. They were driven so that when He turned the throne right side up, there were three nails sticking about half an inch up on the seat of the throne. The Lord spoke to me sternly, "When you sit in the seat of authority I have given you, and you need to feel My nails in your behind to judge rightly." When we judge and criticize incorrectly, we are removed from the ability to stand in a great place of authority.

Round 5: Surviving the Snakes of Church

Zechariah 3:7 says it best: "Thus says the Lord of hosts: 'If you will walk in My ways, and if you will keep My command, then you shall also judge My house, and likewise have charge of My courts; I will give you places to walk among these who stand here.'"

> **When we judge and criticize incorrectly, we are removed from the ability to stand in a great place of authority.**

Scripture is crystal clear. You must walk in His ways and obey Him, and then you can judge. You can then move in the heavenly realms, which are the courts of heaven and walk among them (in the realms of the kingdom!).

It Starts at the Head

During my time at Trinity, it became apparent that some in upper leadership were having moral issues and crises in their Christian walk. I'm still amazed today that out of the multitudes of leadership and some on staff, I only know of a few who did not have a display of backsliding or going back to worldly things. Worldly temptation does start from the head down, and will most likely affect every member of the congregation somehow. It will expose your weaknesses or confirm your strengths.

Needless to say, Trinity was crumbling from the foundation it was built upon. God still had His hand on it; the plans for Trinity and the calling of the city were going to be fulfilled.

> For the time has come for judgment to begin at the house of God; and if it begins with us first, what will be the end of those who do not obey the gospel of God? (1 Peter 4:17).

Fifteen years later, I'm still amazed at the number of leaders who are still bitter, wounded, and resentful about what happened at Trinity.

Church Fathers vs Kingdom Sons

We have a city full of twenty and thirty-year-olds who witnessed, as children and teenagers, the total collapse and restoration. They use it as an excuse not to go to church or be part of any church, and they remain on the outside looking in.

(I am pleased to report Trinity is doing very well, and has recovered to be the lighthouse of God's grace to the city of Deltona and the region.)

Keeping a Kingdom Focus

Twelve years later, on Father's Day weekend in 2010, I had the opportunity to restore this minister to the pulpit. His hair grew back, and he still is one of the best preachers I have ever heard.

Surprisingly, some of the leadership of our city was still angry and resentful and did not want to participate in this restoration process. Even some of my closest friends and associates who had heard for over 12 years that the Lord had given me this mandate to restore him, were starting to question in their hearts whether or not they could participate that weekend.

> And we know that all things work together for good to those who love God, to those who are the called according to His purpose (Romans 8:28).

This verse has to be my all-time kingdom reference verse of Scripture. If I had not gone through this season of my life and learned what I learned, I would not be where I am today. So many times, the Lord teaches by example not only what not to do, but what you're supposed to do and how to do it. At this time in my walk, I began to see how authority in the church system flows from the pastoral office down. The pastor is at the top; everyone submits to him; everyone pours into his vision. If you get out of line or sideways with him, he is obligated to let you know who is boss, even if God is speaking to you.

Round 5: Surviving the Snakes of Church

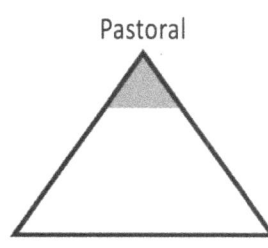

It started becoming pretty clear to me that the fivefold ministry was talked about but never truly honored or engaged. In the church system, with a pastoral position on top, everyone submits only to the vision of the house. Protecting, covering, encouraging, and bringing people through their issues are all necessary portions that the church needs to continue to do. But, without kingdom focus, it can become controlling and religious, and then cause the church to miss the purpose to which God called it.

Please hear me clearly. I believe in authority structures. I believe in the authority of the pastor, and I believe in the authority within the church. But top-down-only leadership can become abusive and detrimental to your spiritual growth and development.

***

Kingdom Keys:

1. God will never release you to pronounce judgment unless you're willing to walk with the person to bring healing and wholeness if there is repentance.
2. There is no greater sin than to commit the sin that was committed against you.

Round 6

The Word of Faith Church

> Behold the proud, his soul is not upright in him; but the just shall live by his faith (Habakkuk 2:4).

When I moved to the Word of Faith Church in Orange City, I met Pastor Carlos**. A six-foot-four, 255-pound ex-con who learned to box while in prison, he went to Rhema Bible School, married, and had several kids. He was by far one of the best Bible teachers I've ever sat under. He did "line by line, precept upon precept" and knew the Word.

When I walked in Pastor Carlos's office and told him that God had sent me to his church, the first thing he did was look at his calendar and start giving the dates that I would be ministering from the pulpit. He said the Lord had told him that a man was coming who needed some pulpit time.

The faithfulness of God to open doors where no man can continues to blow my mind.

During the time that God used Pastor Carlos to open doors for me to minister, I had an encounter with the Holy Spirit one weekend. I was driving my van and listening to a teaching tape on generational curses while going back to Vero Beach to work on one of my rental properties. In the middle of the teaching, the Lord spoke and said, "Do you believe generational CURSES are biblical?"

"Yes, Lord, scripturally I can back that up."

Church Fathers vs Kingdom Sons

He continued, "Do you believe that generational BLESSINGS are biblical also?"

"Yes, I see that You are a generational God all through Scripture."

At that moment, the Lord asked if I wanted the ministry mantle that my grandfather had walked in. My grandfather Coker died when my dad was only eleven years old, so I had no personal revelation of who he was or what he was. The only details I had were from the stories my father told me. Dad told me that one day my grandfather's boss had given him a German hunting knife for protection when he went to preach. My grandfather evidently preached a message of holiness that angered most of the religious people of his day.

I don't know if he ever had to use the knife for protection. But the story always scared me. I asked the Lord if this mantle was a blessing from Him; if it was rightfully mine, could I have it? The Lord told me my grandfather was a prophet to America, so I asked for his mantle.

Kingdom Key: If you don't value your earthly inheritance, you won't redeem it completely for the next generation, nor will you discover your heavenly inheritance.

Too Hard to Keep Clean

I did not realize that that weekend was going to be an encounter with God about that mantle. I had had the same tenant in a rental house for over nine years. As I started to clean the house, I saw it was absolutely trashed. The renter had kept her dog in the garage, and it had urinated and pooped all over the floor. Trying to clean the mess up, I bleached the floor and tried to get the smell out of the garage, but it wasn't working. I drove to the paint store and asked how to seal the concrete and get rid of

Round 6: The Word of Faith Church

that horrible stink. The paint expert told me that I needed to use a two-part epoxy paint that came in three colors: gray, white, and red.

I was halfway through painting the floor when the Holy Spirit invaded the garage. The Lord began to berate me about the stench. He said, "The stench in this house is your fault! You've known for nine years that she had this dog, and you have a lease-contract that said no dogs were allowed. But since she paid her rent on time, you overlooked what was written in your contract. Don't start complaining about the stench in this house when you were the one who allowed it to begin with."

He went on, "You're just like many of My preachers. Just because someone pays their tithes and gives offerings, church leaders don't enforce My written contract. They overlook scriptural principles because of their own comforts. If you're going to be my minister, you better keep to the written contract.

"Look at the paint you're using, trying to seal the smell out. You had three choices of color: red, white, or gray. You didn't choose red because red is too offensive. And you didn't choose white, because white is too hard to keep clean, so you chose gray. That's just like many of my ministers, who don't preach on My blood because it's too offensive; and fewer still preach on holiness because it's too hard to keep clean. They just gray it out and then wonder where the power is.

"If you're going to be My voice, you'd better preach on My blood and preach on a lifestyle of holiness through Me."

At this point I was crying so hard I had tears and snot flowing all over my paint job, all the while asking the Holy Spirit to teach me how to be His voice. The Lord told me to go to a certain church on the north side of Vero Beach, up on the sand ridge. While I sat in the parking lot of this church, asking God why I was sitting here, the church secretary pulled up and asked who I was and what I was doing. I told her that the Lord had been speaking to me about this church while I was praying.

Church Fathers vs Kingdom Sons

She invited me to go into the sanctuary and spend some time at the altar and said she would let me know when she was leaving for the day. After about thirty minutes of getting downloads from the Lord at the altar, the secretary told me she needed to leave and asked my name. I gave her a business card.

As she pulled out of the parking lot, the Holy Spirit said to me, "Look over that fence." To my amazement, on the backside was a cemetery. I walked through the cemetery and found my grandfather's grave. At the grave, I knelt down, cried out to God, and begged Him to give me everything in my generational line that was a blessing. I also asked Him to show me everything in my generational line that was a curse so I could confront it and be productive in the kingdom.

I went into a vision and was shown why my grandmother always prayed to see my father's last child. The day I was born, my grandmother came to the hospital, anointed me with oil, prayed over me and blessed me, and asked God to use me for the kingdom. The following day, she died. I know that's always been a joke in our family, since my dad always said I was so ugly that I killed his mama. God also showed me that because of the fear of man, and the church system, my father was unwilling to walk in the mantle. So my grandmother carried it all those years, and she handed it to me by the power of her blessing.

It's funny that my grandfather was a prophet, and yet was also a member of the Ku Klux Klan. I had discovered the root issues of my own bigotry, the answer to one of the roots of the generational sins of prejudice and racism.

But it takes some willingness to do a little boxing, when necessary, to apply the curse-breaking power of the blood.

My father became upset with me because of the sin I was exposing in our family. But one day in the prison ministry where Dad was working, the Lord demonstrated to him that he had an ongoing problem with racism and needed to repent. I believe that Lord told him if he wasn't going to deal with his heart on this issue, that God would not be able to use him in

Round 6: The Word of Faith Church

ministry. I can tell you that in all the years since, he has been a blessing to African Americans. He has had many of their pictures on his refrigerator, so he can pray for and brag on them. Some, who have come out of the jail and prison, are doing ministry today and when they run into him, they are so grateful. That's called redeeming your family line.

The Power of 4:44 a.m.

The pastor of that church on the north side of Vero Beach, Pastor Frank**, called me a few days after spending time alone at the church's altar. The Lord spoke to him after his secretary gave him my card that afternoon. (I didn't know at the time that after my oldest son was born, Susie was attending this pastor's church and that he had dedicated Jason.) This pastor completely opened up his heart and his church for me to minister. God was opening up doors that no man could open. Pastor Frank had become the elder at the gate of Vero Beach for me, even though it is the place of my father's birth and mine. He was the apostolic doorway for me personally. I never ministered in Vero without letting him know where and when.

I was starting to operate in an extremely high level of the prophetic, with no formal training but with an extreme zeal for God. I was developing a reputation in our community as a prophet. Well, in the church system that's not a good reputation to have, since there is very little room for that kind of gift. God developed the skill set in us, therefore it is up to us to expand the kingdom.

God started waking me up at 4:44 a.m. every morning for weeks and weeks. When He woke me up, He would say, "You're my prophet. Don't be discouraged."

Finally, one morning I yelled, "What are you trying to tell me?"

Then He said, "You finally asked? So look up John 4:44: 'For Jesus Himself testified that a prophet has no honor in his own country.' And don't let rejection control your love walk." So when I get depressed He starts waking me up at 4:44 a.m., and then I stop pouting.

Church Fathers vs Kingdom Sons

Strong Personalities

We did ministry with a lot of people during this season, but one couple that stands out was George and Judy Jones. Judy was the best kids' minister in the county, and she was hungry for truth. God showed me that her daughter was sneaking out of her house at night and doing wrong stuff. Judy was offended because she thought her family was perfect and that prophets were only to give words of edification. But it was a clear, direct word for her family. She told George, and he confirmed to her that it was true. When she called to thank me, it started a relationship of trust, even if it was hard at times.

Judy is a strong, gifted woman of God. She has a great calling, but she had some control areas that made us butt heads a lot. Every time Judy would come to a crossroads with God, He would tell her to call me.

I never offered her nice, flowery words. It was always very blunt and to the point. "You need to learn to submit to your husband! You're in rebellion in this area. Judy, I see you jumping on a springboard of impatience into a pool of disobedience," I've said. Her strong personality (another word for control) is something I understand quite well, since I was born into a family with three older sisters. (I was the only boy, the baby, and my mother's favorite. Plus, I was born on her birthday.) They tried to kill me most of the time. So, as a result of my upbringing, I don't baby women. Judy is one of the reasons God gave me that training. If you want to box like a man, get in the ring, put on your big-girl panties, and let's rumble!

Kingdom Key: When you rumble in love, You can live in peace in the Kingdom.

My time at the Word of Faith Church was critical, since the scandals at Trinity were capturing the people's attention. National and local media were having a field day exposing all of the corruption within the church. The problem is, it's the people who get hurt. Multitudes of them

Round 6: The Word of Faith Church

were running from God because of what they saw and heard outside church walls.

Thrown Out of the Office

Many a night I would walk and pray over our city and ask God to heal us. All the while, God was teaching me how to operate in my gifting. He was teaching me to be gracious, loving, and kind, and at the same time bring revelatory information to leaders who, many times, did not want it. We began to host revival meetings with some of the traveling ministers who had flocked to Florida because of the revival that broke out in Lakeland with Howard-Browne.

The joy of the Lord was needed very much in our region and churches. That anointing is still very important to my walk. Joy is one of the signs of the kingdom: righteousness, peace, and joy in the Holy Ghost.

One night in prayer, the Lord gave me a revelation that Pastor Carlos needed help battling a demonic spirit that was being empowered by his wife. (Jezebel) The Lord gave me very clear instructions to go to him and let him know it was time to deal with the situation.

The next day, I went by the church office to see Pastor Carlos. I spoke plainly: "Pastor, the Lord has given me a word for you." I started to give the revelation to him, but he did not receive it. This six-foot-four, 255-pound man got physical with me, picked me up, and basically tossed me out of his office.

I was completely shocked with what had just gone down! To clear my head, I went for a ride in the woods to get alone with God. I cried out to the Lord, "Why did it happen this way? Why did You let this happen to me? I thought You sent me! I thought he would receive me! I thought this was going to be a coming together and healing would happen."

After twenty minutes of a major hissy fit, God gave me an additional word. He said for me to go back to see Pastor Carlos the next morning. I was to tell him that while I was not the first prophet He had sent to him with this word, I was the last; and that if he did not deal with the situation in forty days, God was going to close the doors to his church.

The next morning I went as the Lord instructed me, and I sat with Pastor Carlos. I said, "After the events of yesterday, I got alone with God to find out if I had missed it; if I had, I was going to come here and repent." I calmly told him what that the Lord had spoken to me the previous day, emphasizing the forty-day time limit that the Lord gave to change what was wrong.

The answer he gave shocked me. "No, you're not the first; but we'll see if you're the last."

Forty days later, the landlord decided not to renew the lease and the church shut its doors.

Faking the Gift

One of the last times I ministered at that church, I was operating at a very high level in words of knowledge, down to very small details of people's lives. After I got home from the meeting, I tried to rest. The Lord wanted to debrief me about what went on during ministry time. As God clarified some things that I should have said or not said, He asked if I knew how the gift worked. I told Him I was getting used to it, and I was starting to feel confident. The Lord said that He was pleased with my love for the gift, but it was His and not mine. And then told me He was going to take it from me for a season. I asked why, and He said that I didn't have the character to sustain a gift of that caliber.

It seemed like the light bulb was turned off; and I can tell you that from that day on, I was not very confident with personal prophecy. But when I am on an assignment, I will get what I need from the Lord to do what He tells me to do. I still see regional and corporate stuff. To this day, I operate at about 15 percent of what I did when He was training me. Personal prophecy is still the weakest part of my gifting.

Round 6: The Word of Faith Church

I remember about six weeks after the gift was turned off, I walked up to three ladies who were standing and talking. I gave them a look and made a moaning sound, trying to make them think God had shown me stuff. With that, one lady started repenting for things that she thought I knew.

When I got home, the Lord threatened to end my earthly existence if I ever did that again. It was then that I got mad and told Him that this gift had given me a reputation. It was hard not living up to my reputation. Sternly He spoke, "I will give the gift back to you if your church reputation is more important than kingdom integrity. Or, you can be like Me and have no reputation." At that point, I became the chief spokesman for the kingdom.

Kingdom Key: You can lose your reputation and still maintain your integrity in the kingdom.

Almost 2 years later, Pastor Carlos came to my store and asked me to support him financially in a Bible school that he was starting. I asked one question: "Have you dealt with the situation that the Lord revealed to you?" He said, "No. I've been afraid to deal with that situation, because I don't want to lose my wife."

> For I have told him [Eli] that I will judge his house forever for the iniquity *which he knows*, because his sons made themselves vile, and he did not restrain them" (1 Samuel 3:13, emphasis added).

It's amazing how the fear of man forces tremendously gifted ministers to abort their true destinies and callings. I'm sad to say that a year later, Pastor Carlos committed suicide. He was extremely instrumental in my growth on my own personal journey, and for that I am grateful.

The kingdom expands!

Church Fathers vs Kingdom Sons

Called to a Man

I felt a stirring in my spirit; something new was changing this time. My paradigm was shifting from just viewing the kingdom in the spiritual realm to wanting to walk more in the fullness of it in the natural. I was starting to resent the systems of the church that I felt were bringing death and destruction to her people. If God had let me, I would've completely escaped the church system, but it was not in God's plan at that time.

As I was studying in 1 Samuel about Eli the priest, the Lord spoke to me. "You're going to make a move. I will no longer send you to a church; I will send you to a man." Hallelujah, hallelujah!"

I thought this would be an amazing change. If God sent me to a man instead of a church system, the man would undoubtedly receive me. He might become a spiritual father to me, or a mentor, perhaps even helping me in my calling instead of trying to prostitute my gift within his church system.

Returning to Romans 8:28: "God works all things out."

It is amazing how many people I was in ministry with then who I'm now still doing ministry with today. My friend Rodger, who was the children's pastor at Trinity, called me one day and said, "Hey, I have been promoted to associate pastor. You have to come and meet our new pastor."

The meeting was set up, and I went to the meeting hoping that he had a heart to restore all the damage had been done to the church body in that city. What a monumental task this would be!

On the morning that we met, the Lord spoke to me. "Remember, I told you I was sending you to a man, not to a church." As I walked in the door and met the new pastor of Trinity, the Lord said, "This is the man. He is my priest; submit to him, come alongside him, and help him heal this church and the city."

Round 6: The Word of Faith Church

Susie and I had been traveling as itinerant ministers for over a year at that point. We came and got involved. Very quickly, we found our place to serve and began forming and rebuilding relationships.

The Lord had definitely sent this man and gifted him with the skill set, I believe, to get the job done. God had given him a vision that he was to be a Joshua. He would cross over the Jordan and bring this church into the Promised Land. Here I was, back at Trinity, helping to rebuild it from the foundation up. I was doing my part: traveling, running my business, and trying to keep a household intact.

***

Kingdom Keys:

1. If you don't value your earthly inheritance, you won't redeem it completely for the next generation, nor will you discover your heavenly inheritance.
2. When you rumble in love, You can live in peace in the kingdom.
3. You can lose your reputation and still maintain your integrity in the kingdom.

Round 7

Being Sent to a Man, Not a Church

When I had the vision about God hardening the men's hearts, it was no surprise that Pastor Joe** was on the list. He was a man I loved and for whom I was willing to lay down my life and ministry. I strove to please him so that I could win his favor.

I have to say that if my father had been a full-time pastor covering a church, he would've been a twin to Pastor Joe—same skill set and personality to boot. If I had known then what I know now, I might have handled the situation differently. However, I can never be certain since I was an orphan striving to be accepted, constantly striving to please Papa God, with a deep longing in my soul to be spiritually fathered. Problem is, Pastor Joe was a spiritual orphan just like my natural father. When two orphans are in the same house, there's usually trouble.

Trinity was beginning to turn around. But with so many people hurt, leadership had to be sensitive to the pace of the changes they sought to implement. Pastor Joe was a revivalist at heart, and the church was Pentecostal. Best pay attention to the speed bumps ahead! Once the church started settling down from the crisis it had gone through, we got used to new leadership and their styles, function, and gifting. God was starting to show up!

A Watchman on the Wall

One Sunday morning, I was sitting in my second-row pew in my fancy "leadership" suit. The Holy Spirit asked me directly, "Are you a prophet?"

I replied, "Lord, you said I am."

He fired back, "I need a prophet on the wall today."

Pastor was midway through a message and preaching when the Lord told me to go stand by a 25-foot tree that stood between the altar and the seats. I had been standing by the wall next to this tree, asking the Lord what He wanted me to do. He answered: "You are a watchmen on the wall—watch this. I need you to watch what I'm about to do."

All of a sudden, a wind of the Holy Spirit blew into the room. Pastor stopped speaking, and people came to the altar and got saved, healed, and delivered.

This started happening on such a regular basis that Pastor Rodger** and others were told to take their positions on the opposite wall. It became obvious that God was going to move when we stood in our positions, so I asked the Lord what He was trying to accomplish.

The Lord said, "I am offering this church and its leadership an opportunity to function within the fivefold ministry. I'm asking you to birth the prophetic and to submit to the ones I send."

Pastor Joe understood the fivefold ministry well, but he did have a problem with its function. It's one thing to have an understanding of something, but it's another to let it function around you. Could he allow it to function and flourish around him?

We started holding huge River Conferences and having some of the stars of the charismatic zoo coming to the house. The speakers who came were extremely high caliber and traveled on the revival circuit at

Round 7: Being Sent to a Man, Not a Church

the time. We were drawn into a season where we had extended meetings, and God was moving in a powerful way.

Favor in New York

At this time, I was still traveling regularly to New York. I would fly into Buffalo, rent a car, and then drive two hours south of Rochester to Hornell. I had been doing this for several years after the Lord showed me a vision about a coming move of His glory across this nation. He would send me to the triangular-shaped region there, and the anointing was tangible when I was within the triangle of responsibility. God always showed me who the elders were at the gates of each city within the region.

> ## Many want authority but will not take responsibility.

Many want authority but will not take responsibility. The Lord said if I would come once a month, He would teach me how the kingdom of God works in the heavenly and then how it transfers to the earthly arenas. So, once a month I would fly into Buffalo, drive into the little towns, repent for the sins of the churches and leadership of each town, and ask God for revival and healing. All the while, God was teaching me about how kingdom functions and how the apostolic works within those principles.

On one trip God asked who I thought were the apostolic leaders of Hornell. We started talking about different leaders, and He then said that I would not be able to find them from the ground. So I rented an airplane to fly over Hornell. As the Lord showed me a church next to an old warehouse, He said to go find her. He had a word for her.

When I found the church, they were having an outing in the park down the road. I found the pastor, who introduced herself as Mother

Church Fathers vs Kingdom Sons

Brasswell. I gave her the word from the Lord about her being an apostolic leader in the city.

She told me that for twenty-six years she had been pastor of this church in Hornell but she lived in Niagara Falls, a two-hour drive away. She related how she'd watched all the big-time ministries come and grow large and then be taken out of the game by the enemy. She knew God had directed her to live somewhere else.

I told her that the Lord would not let her live under the great oppression that was over this little city. This city is a spiritual switchgear. It was the same thing in the natural when the Erie Railroad maintenance shops were there in Hornell. The blueprint seen on earth is the mirror of what is in heaven. This revelation has been vital for understanding how long to stay in a region and not be detected by the enemy. Mother Brasswell is still at her post as I write this book. She has to be over ninety and is still kicking the devil's butt.

God had shown me favor with some of the most influential leaders of that region. The Lord told me to go see Pastor Reid from The Tabernacle in Orchard Park, south of Buffalo. As He opened doors for me to preach at The Tab, it was a public sign of favor in the region. Pastor Reid is a true statesman in the kingdom. He would put me up in a house that the church owned on Prayer Mountain. He had me preach several times on Sunday nights. He was the one who had me preach the first service on a Sunday morning, with Tommy Tenney preaching the second service. It was Favor.

One day, I asked the Lord where the favor came from. He reminded me that I had asked for the generational blessings from my grandfather on my dad's side, and I got his prophetic mantle. I thought that there might be some unused blessings on my dad's side, so instead I asked for any and all blessings that were legally mine from my mother's side.

Later I learned that the favor I was receiving came from the Albrecht family. Back in 1945, when this church was only a storefront in the city of Buffalo, the Albrecht family was in the Mennonite denomination.

Round 7: Being Sent to a Man, Not a Church

They had gotten filled with the Holy Ghost. Grandpa Albrecht had thirteen children. Every year they would sell Christmas trees and ask God who the family should bless with the money as their family offering. I discovered this information when a lady at the church came to me after I preached and asked if I was Onalee Rigby's son. I told her yes and then watched as the pieces of the puzzle came together.

See, my mother got saved at thirteen and would go to the church camp up near Buffalo, where she met and was spiritually adopted as an Albrecht; my mother and several of the Albrecht girls were lifelong friends. When the Albrecht family moved to Florida, my mother wrote a letter to Aunt Ruth and told her that this was the last winter she was going to sleep in the cold; when she got to Florida she was going to find a husband.

In the summer of 1948, there was a tent meeting held in Vero Beach with a female evangelist; and once my father and some of his friends showed up, well … the rest is history. From that revival, the church in Vero Beach was birthed.

The favor that came from asking for the generational blessing has blown my mind. My mother was not of an earthly line but of a spiritual line. You can get generational blessing from the spiritual relationship, This is how the kingdom works.

Honoring the Man of God

While on a ministry trip, I was going up a hill in a rented Ford Explorer. I pushed the car to its limit as the hill gradually steepened. When I topped the hill, the Holy Spirit spoke to me and said, "You wouldn't treat your vehicle that way, but because this is a rental, you have no problem abusing it." He started relating my abuse of this rental car to the grief that I was giving Pastor Joe. The Lord said that I was treating him like a "rent-a-pastor" and that I had better straighten up and fly right and start honoring him.

Church Fathers vs Kingdom Sons

I had a vision, and He showed me why I was so frustrated with Pastor Joe. In this vision, the Lord helped me understand that Pastor's whole life had been preparation for this season. He had been prepared to function as an apostle and a spiritual father to the body of Christ. God showed me great details, and how the devil had exposed the sin of the church in the last season, even at a national level. If Pastor Joe functioned as an apostle in his leadership, God was going to release a billboard of His grace. This church would be a sign and a wonder, and it would represent the kingdom and all of its glory.

Just I was finishing this encounter with the Lord, my cell phone rang—and it was Pastor Joe, asking when I was coming home. He told me that they had extended the meeting another week and that the Lord told him to have me preach on Monday night. I told him that I had just been given a word and that I could be back in town late Monday afternoon and could preach Monday night.

That night, I prophesied with profound accuracy (his words) for forty-five minutes. I publicly declared that he was an apostle. However, he had been unwilling to function as one, since his apostolic gift was not honored in the system into which he was birthed: only his role as pastor was honored and recognized. I explained that Satan had made a spectacle out of the church at the national level, and God wanted to make this church a billboard of His grace for the world to see. The Lord said that Pastor would have to take the church out of its denomination and become independent; then he would be able to function in the fivefold ministry at the level to which he was called. The Lord revealed that in forty days, on Mother's Day, a new movement would begin. That night I charged leadership to judge the word.

Pastor and the leadership came into agreement. They made 350 tapes of the prophecy and handed them out the following Sunday. He also called a fast for the forty days until the Mother's Day service.

Mother's Day came, and Pastor Joe called nine different leaders who had been functioning in their ministries to the altar. For the first time as

Round 7: Being Sent to a Man, Not a Church

an apostle, he prophesied over us, laid hands on us, and commissioned us to fulfill the calling on our lives. It was profound for the Lord to pick Mother's Day. I believe the Brownsville revival, which impacted the world, was birthed on Father's Day and was a restoration of what was old. But this fivefold ministry birth needed to be on Mother's Day because it was a birthing of a new movement.

A New Mentor

Over the next few months my traveling ministry started to take off. I was seeing great unity in the cities and churches where I was preaching, and I was starting to bring churches and ministries together corporately.

I was finally starting to see some fulfillment of the promises God had given me. Returning home from one of my trips, as the pastor was preaching, a man I didn't know was standing next to "my" tree at church. This guy looked like a sergeant major in the army. I asked the Lord who this person was. The Lord said to me, "He is a senior prophet, and I have sent him here because you have cried and whined about wanting a mentor. He is now your authority in the prophetic. Submit to him."

I went and introduced myself to Alex. I told him who he was in the kingdom, that God had told me to submit to him, and that he was to be my mentor. There was a little problem, though ... we didn't like each other very much. For over a year, I felt as if all he ever did was give me instructions and a hard time. He loved Pastor Rodger, and that ticked me off a lot.

One Thursday morning, Pastor Rodger asked me to come and teach chapel at the school. Just before I began to speak, Alex came to me and said he had a word from the Lord. He said God told him that I was arrogant and prideful, that I had offended my pastor, and that I needed to repent. As soon as I was done teaching chapel, I went to the pastor's office and said, "Pastor, I'm arrogant, prideful, and if I have offended you, please forgive me." He said that to his knowledge he had not been offended, and he didn't believe any of those issues were true.

Church Fathers vs Kingdom Sons

As I left the office, I found Alex waiting in the hallway. He asked, "Did you repent the way I told you to?" I said, "Yes, but Pastor didn't know anything was wrong and said we were good. I repented anyway." He started walking down the hall with an attitude, so I asked what his problem was. He let me know that he had told God that he would not mentor someone unless he would blindly obey him with no questions asked: I passed that test. He only mentored me by demand, and for the next few years it was like oil and water. He had a great gift but was a horse's behind. But I honored his gift and wanted what he had.

The problem with Alex and me is that we were both heavily gifted orphans.

Just a side note. A few years later, the Lord told me to call Alex and tell him I had a word for his church. I told God, "He can hear you; if you want me to preach in his church, have him call me."

That night, Alex called. "The Lord told me that you're stubborn. You wouldn't call me and tell me you had a word to preach."

I sent out an email to the locals about preaching on Thursday night at his church. The crowd was so much larger than normal, his wife said that I should be the pastor. LOL.

When Alex stood up to introduce me, he said, "I'll tell you what I like about Charlie Coker…" It was as if he froze in place, and the cat got his tongue. After forty-five seconds, he started looking hard at his paper to find something good to say about me. At that point I yelled, "It's okay, Alex. Everybody knows we respect each other, but we don't get along." He regained his composure and told everyone that he admired me in spite of myself because no matter what, I never stop pursuing God. Ironically, I spoke on offenses!

Stealing Money to Give to the Priest

I began to sense that God was about to birth something new within me; He began with the River Conferences and extended meetings for

Round 7: Being Sent to a Man, Not a Church

revival. Could it be that the King who had walked through the wall, changed my heart, and introduced Himself to me as a supernatural God, would begin to show me His kingdom in a greater dimension? I began to feel that my days of usefulness at this church were coming to an end.

Charlie Coker, the businessman, had written large checks to support those conferences, which served to birth revival. The more checks I wrote, the more my pastor would say, "You can't out-give God." He urged me to give more, even though my company was struggling. "Give, keep on giving, and give by faith."

One Sunday morning, the checkbook looked dismal and the pressure to quit had come to the point of a showdown. So instead of going to church that morning, I went to my office and grabbed a phonebook and the Bible. I threw both of the books on the floor and told God one of these two books was going to give me an answer about the future for my business and me. "You can speak to me through Your Word, or I will find an attorney in this phonebook. I will file for bankruptcy and quit the business."

The Lord spoke to me and told me to go to Psalm 107:27–28: "They reel to and fro, and stagger like a drunken man, and are at their wits' end. Then they cry out to the Lord in their trouble and He brings them out of their distresses."

> **A church priest will continue to put demands on you, even when you're out of balance. Kingdom fathers get involved and make sure you're in balance.**

Man, I was at my wit's end! I pleaded with the Lord and asked Him to deliver me from my distress. He gave me a very clear word: "Charlie, you have stolen money from your vendors and have given the money to the priest. You think it is blessed, because the priest said so. I consider that money stolen." He ordered me to go through my vender invoice files, call out their names one by one, and repent for stealing their money and giving it to the priests. The Lord then told me not to sow finances out of the business until my company was paying its bills on time.

Susie and I began tithing and giving offerings only from the salaries we took home. A church priest will continue to put demands on you, even when you're out of balance. Kingdom fathers get involved and make sure you're in balance.

Let me put a disclaimer on this: I believe in tithing and giving. I believe that there are times that God will ask you to supernaturally sacrifice and give. You must hear the voice of God and not be manipulated by man.

Rejecting the Prophetic Word

Pastor Joe called me into his office about six months after I had given the prophecy about Mother's Day. He said the most unusual thing to me. I'll never forget it. He said, "Charlie, I believe that was the word of the Lord, and that is His perfect will. But if I take this church out of this denomination, we will lose too many people, and I have chosen not to do it." After that I got up, shook his hand, and told him that I was going to obey God to the best of my ability, because I was promised that I would be a billboard of His grace. I thought it would be by working beside him in ministry, but I was wrong.

I remember sharing the mandate with Pastor Joe about how God asked me to be instrumental in restoring the former pastor back to the pulpit when his hair grew back, but instead of helping me, he would start churning inside. I know how challenging it is to work at restoring someone when you were the one who had to clean up the mess left behind.

At times I would ask, "Pastor, have you forgiven him?" and he would give a flippant answer. I would tell him, "Biblical forgiveness means coming with a verbal request that isn't lip service and a physical willingness to restore or repay. Are you sure you have forgiven?" When I finally did restore the former pastor in 2010, Pastor Joe was my worst critic. He totally missed the kingdom principle. That's what orphans do.

Round 7: Being Sent to a Man, Not a Church

Confronting "Ahab" and "Jezebel"

I had a really bad situation with a pastor in New York who was an elder at the gates of Hornell for me. I had built relationships with him for years, and personally, we were good friends. I was well received by his congregation. We held multicongregational meetings and were starting to network at a regional level, and I had come to speak in a three-day engagement.

Friday night, the Saturday morning with the men, and Saturday night were all great, strong meetings. But early Sunday morning, the Lord woke me up and gave me a word that I knew was correction, direction, and even a warning. I gave a copy of the message to the pastor, and he approved it. As I spoke, I went into a vision and was shown that the destiny of that church was hanging in the balance. I started to weep, tried to explain the severity of the message that I was releasing, and even predicted that leadership marriages would come to divorce. I mentioned that the church would have to close its doors if they didn't respond to the Lord. The whole message was about God changing the language of the pastor and for him to speak with kindness to others.

> **True covenant will always be personally costly.**

I had made a covenant relationship with this man. God had always given me a very good revelation about covenant. I knew from my experiences that true covenant will always be personally costly. As an example, look at the covenant that God made with Abraham in Genesis 15:7–18. God took a bull, cut it in half, and walked between both halves. I know that when I am told to make a covenant, the Cut the Bull anointing will show up.

I make covenant totally intent on God's perfect will. If those with whom I make a covenant are only interested in God's permissive will, a crisis always occurs in the relationship, and the covenant becomes severed. But sometimes it's time to "cut the bull" and then hear God say His promises to us like He did Abram. The "ham," or name change, was not added until the test of the covenant was completed: "On the same day the Lord made a covenant with Abraham" (Genesis 15:18).

You would think that it wouldn't be a big deal, right? But two weeks later when I was called to his house, two board members, his wife, and he had decided to persuade me to retract what I'd said. Being the orphan that I was, I decided to challenge them, since I felt bullied and pushed into a corner. As the discussion escalated even further, I called him an Ahab and her a Jezebel.

My comments were not wrong; I was just not wise doing it in that situation and to their faces. One thing led to another, and my own battling orphan spirit wanted to defend my identity as a prophet. Had I had been mature I would've agreed, repented, and walked away; but I didn't. They had a prophet on staff who decided to challenge me. To make a long story short, most of the fruitful ministry I had been doing in New York came to a screeching halt. I got so mad that I wrote letters to the board members at their church. I let them know, in no uncertain terms, that I was willing to fly from Florida, meet them in the town square, let the God who answers by fire show up, and kill the one who was wrong. I reacted this way because my identity had become wrapped up in my gifting. This little escapade cost me relationships with some of the biggest churches in the region. Even though I felt justified, I should have asked the Lord for the right words, since mine weren't received well.

As I drove back to the Buffalo airport, I was completely devastated and asked God what happened. He reprimanded me for how I had put this relationship above the covenant with Him and had put too much responsibility on man and not on Him. I felt like I would never fulfill my calling or see the promise of revival.

Round 7: Being Sent to a Man, Not a Church

Trying to Repair the Damage

Pastor Joe and Alex made me cancel my travel schedule for the rest of the year. I needed that time away to heal and learn some life lessons. As I cried about the New York region of ministry, God told me to let it die and said that if I would do that, I would reap the increase of other regions. One of my prophet friends told this story in a book he wrote on what to never do in ministry. Never tell a woman to her face that she is a Jezebel and that her husband is an Ahab. They will murder you.

Everything came crashing apart, and I really didn't want to return to New York. Pastor Reid from the Buffalo area was preaching at one of the River Conferences and asked me where I had been. I assumed that he had heard what had happened between me and the pastor in Hornell. Pastor Reid took me aside and fathered me at a very critical time in ministry. He said he had heard what happened and that he had also heard I had repented a few times. "I never thought you were a quitter," he said sadly. "The pastor is a hot-headed Italian from the Bronx, and he may never forgive you. I believe what God showed you about revival is from Him." He prayed for me and asked me to let him know when I was coming back to New York.

Over the last twelve years, I've sat down seven different times and tried to repair this broken relationship. First I went as a young immature prophet, then as a traveling evangelist, and finally as a maturing apostle. I got so tired of repenting; it started to make me sick, until one day the Lord showed me Matthew 5:23–25 (emphasis added):

> Therefore if you bring your *gift* to the altar, and there remember that your *brother* has something against you, leave your *gift* there before the altar, and go your way. First be reconciled to your *brother*, and then come and offer your *gift*. Agree with your adversary quickly, while you are on the way with him, lest your adversary deliver you to the judge, the judge hand you over to the officer, and you be thrown into prison.

Church Fathers vs Kingdom Sons

Susie has a saying: "When you extend the olive branch of peace, make sure it still has leaves on it, or it's just a stick and brings more wounds."

The Lord spoke to me about the fivefold ministry, which are gifts found in the book of Ephesians. Yet they are not greater than the relationship with a brother. If we would lay our ministry titles down and reconcile with our brother first, maybe we could start manifesting the kingdom and not some hierarchal system that brings death rather than life. The last time I met with this pastor, I met as a brother truly concerned about him as a brother and not a minister. "They will know them for their love, one for another." After that last meeting, God released me from trying to restore this relationship.

The sad thing to report is that the pastor and his wife are now divorced, and many in their church leadership are struggling with their walk with the Lord. The associate pastor, Terry, and I became very good friends, and after the situation, we walked together. I tried to help him for six years to forgive this pastor and the church system, to no avail. We were accountable to each other as we both pursued God, but Terry would not walk in love and get healed or allow God to remove the bitterness in his heart.

Terry was a strong prophet. We would eventually come to a place in his journey when he needed to repent and forgive, but he guarded his bitterness. Each time he got a toe infection, it remained as an open wound until he repented. This happened at least six different times over several years. Terry eventually got divorced and moved a few hundred miles away.

One day I was talking to him on the phone and asked a very simple question. "Terry, are you living with a woman?" Boy, did that set him over the edge! He wrote me a nasty email telling me I was as judgmental and critical as the old church system was, and he was done with our relationship. I asked the Lord how to respond. He told me to send him an email asking for forgiveness for offending him and invading his personal space and to admit to him that I had not realized our relationship had

Round 7: Being Sent to a Man, Not a Church

changed. Since I could no longer hold him accountable in those areas, I needed his forgiveness.

A few months later, Terry's toe infection came back and he wound up in the hospital. I asked the Lord if I should fly to New York and lay hands on him to heal him. The Lord said, "No; he had his opportunity, and he chose not to walk in forgiveness." A week later, his toe infection spread to his bloodstream, then his heart: and he died. He was fifty years old.

This kingdom principle of love is a must. The Lord gave me a quote to live by: "Charlie, if you cannot love by your standards, you cannot live by them either." This was a hard lesson for me to learn, because in the last season I had become very religious and dogmatic in my belief system. Let me put it in Susie's words: "I had become a religious ass."

Kingdom Key: Love MUST be the standard for operating in the kingdom.

Thrust out of the Church

It came time to leave Trinity. I made up my mind that before I left, Pastor Joe was going to give me his blessing (which he never did). I have been labeled rebellious and not submissive, but I had purposed in my heart that I was going to get his blessing one way or another. So, needless to say, I overstayed my welcome. I told God that if He was going to make me leave without his blessing, I wanted a prophet to call me out publicly and tell me that I wasn't welcome at that church anymore.

One day, Dr. Richardson, a major prophet who had preached at the River Conferences, was leading some meetings at the church. He called me out. He chastised me publicly and said, "You aren't welcome here anymore. You aren't liked, and you are staying here because you covet the blessing of a man. You are in rebellion to God and need to leave."

Church Fathers vs Kingdom Sons

That got me in trouble big-time both with Pastor Joe and Dr. Richardson. Pastor Joe rebuked him, and I had to tell them both that I had forced God's hand. Both of them were mad at me, but I finally got the word I needed. Susie and I started looking for a new church.

It was sad to see that nine leaders who Pastor Joe had released to do what God had told them to do had no relationship with either him or the church after a year. He had missed the greatest opportunity to father, but he craved power and control. All nine of us felt that the control and the top-down system were not the kingdom. But to this day, all of us are in ministry doing what he spoke over us. A few of us are still in ministry with each other.

He's Preaching My Messages!

Out of the nine ministries that were birthed that day, I was the only one who pursued relationship for years. I believe the problem I had is that the Lord had told me that He would send me to a man, not a church or a system, and I was getting really frustrated as I waited. But when one is an orphan, he or she will not have the capacity or understanding to serve as a spiritual father to others. I had a crisis because I knew God had shown me what was supposed to be done, but it was out of my control. God had also told me that revelations and new teachings about the kingdom that I was given would be preached from the pulpit of Trinity. The only problem was I thought it was me that would do the preaching.

Enter one of my employees, Marsha, who went to Trinity. She would hear about my fresh revelations at work, and then I would go have lunch with Pastor Joe and for the next three weeks he would preach my messages from the pulpit.

Man, that would tick me off. I told God one day that it wasn't fair. That's when He told me He was working on my EGO (Edging God Out).

"Are your messages getting preached at Trinity like I told you?"

Round 7: Being Sent to a Man, Not a Church

"Yes, Lord, but I thought if You gave me the revelation that I would be the one preaching it."

"That's your problem—you thought and did not ask. My ways are higher than your ways, remember."

The Builder's Note

My friends came to me, saying that they heard God. He told them that I had to go to a Morningstar Conference. I was in no mood, so I told them if they believed that it was God, they had to pay all my expenses to attend. And they did! I want to share a dream with you that I had while at Morningstar.

In the middle of the first night of the conference, I entered into a prophetic dream. In the dream, I was trying to convince Pastor Joe that I had a $10,000 builder's note, which looked like a stock certificate. I knew it belonged to him and was trying to get him to take possession of it. I had people around who were connected to me and waiting outside that room for me to get rid of this $10,000 builder's note. I debated and argued, but he would not take ownership of the note.

I awoke from the dream, and the Lord spoke to me saying, "What you have is valuable, but you can't force even things of value on someone who does not want it." I went back to sleep and returned to the dream. I revisited him one more time and was arguing and trying to get him to take responsibility and ownership, since it had his name on it. I let him know, "You're an apostle; you're a builder; and this is a $10,000 builder's note," but he would not receive it.

In the dream, people connected to me were starting to get angry with me, since I would not move forward until this note was given to its rightful owner and resolved. Many told me to just keep it myself and stayed out of the line of fire in the hallway as I was arguing with Pastor Joe. Then, all of a sudden, Pastor Rodger came to me and said, "Listen, I've told everybody to give you time and space, because you will not

Church Fathers vs Kingdom Sons

take something that's not rightfully yours. But, Charlie, he's a pastor. Don't make him take ownership; give it to him as a gift."

I answered, "That's a great idea! I will give it to him as a gift."

I returned to the office and I humbly said to Pastor Joe, "I'm giving you this as a gift, free and clear no strings attached." I handed it to him, and he received it with gladness. Then he walked over to the front of his computer, took the certificate and he put it in the front of his computer. The computer sucked it in and a few seconds later spit it back out. It sucked it back in, then spit it back out. Pastor Joe took the certificate, handed it to me, and he made this statement: "My system cannot take this."

I came out of the dream, and the Lord asked, "When are you going to stop trying to make people take ownership of the kingdom system, when they won't put down their church system first? Stop trying to force people." He was planning to open doors, and I had to make a decision and not look back. God said, "No regrets. This is part of your journey."

> Most assuredly, I say to you, unless a grain of wheat falls into the ground and dies, it remains alone; but if it dies, it produces much grain (John 12:24).

Later, at the conference, Rick Joyner introduced a guest speaker who had not been scheduled: Dr. Richardson! I was sitting in the middle of a large crowd, knowing that God had heard my cry. Dr. Richardson called me out by name. He, Jack Deere, and several others spoke a word over me that released me from the old system, and gave me new marching orders for the new system. The word explained why I never seemed to fit in the local church.

I've seen this pastor-driven triangle system long enough to know that it does not work long with kingdom principles. So my journey moves on ...

Round 7: Being Sent to a Man, Not a Church

***

Kingdom Keys:

1. If you cannot love by your standards, you cannot live by them either.
2. Love is the standard for operating in the kingdom.
3. When you extend the olive branch of peace, make sure it still has leaves on it, or it's just a stick and brings more wounds.

Round 8

What Do You Do When Your Reality Check Bounces?

The middle rounds of every good boxing match can be grueling, to say the least. During my journey I think that this was probably the most difficult season.

I had been away from New York for more than two years and really didn't care about going back.

But as the Lord started reminding me of the revival that He showed me, I would get excited all over again. I started to push for God to do something supernatural. He reminded me that I had to regain regional authority by walking back into the area that had murdered me, and ... I had to do it in love.

> **Authority is granted to the ones who take responsibility.**

The devil can't ever handle love. Some I had offended would not forgive and restore me, but God would grant me greater authority IF I continued to take responsibility over the city and region that He had given to me to expand the kingdom. Authority is granted to the ones who take responsibility.

I came out of the last church extremely hurt, wounded, and, to be honest with you, angry at the church system. If God had let me, I would have printed bumper stickers that read "Church Sucks" and put them on every pastor's car I knew. But my King, who is inside of me, wouldn't allow that. Meanwhile, He was giving me revelation on how His kingdom should function, but it just wasn't adding up in the natural.

New Connections in New York

I had been building a strong connection with Apostle Brad** in New York. I began to be exposed to the apostolic and how it functioned within the house church movement. I liked what I heard, I liked what I saw, and it had some of the kingdom principles that I knew God was showing me to walk in.

Apostle Brad and I continued our relationship when I traveled to New York. His ministry was one of prophetic deliverance. Boy, did Susie and I need some of that! His ministry brought more inner healing than anything we had been involved in before. Coming out of the church system, wounded and creating my own problems in New York, I was one big mess.

His team had set up a deliverance session in a hotel room in Buffalo. Ironically, the day before our session, I ran into my aunt in Hornell. During our conversation, she started telling that me that my maternal grandfather used to be in senior leadership in a Masonic lodge. I had never known that!

During the deliverance sessions in Buffalo, a team member had a vision of a demon swinging at me with a high-ranking Masonic ring on its finger. It still amazes me how much garbage we deal with in our generational lines. Just remember: the cross and the blood of Jesus cancel all curses. When the effects of those curses linger, we need to deal with them properly.

I started believing with all my heart that the apostolic system would be the one to replace the church system.

Round 8: What Do You Do When Your Reality Check Bounces?

The problem with this belief system is that we are all of the same family, and because of our differences, we can be at odds with each other. Some of the people in this movement believe that the house church movement is God's new thing, and anything with a building is demonic.

With all my hurts and wounds, I became like Saul before he became Paul. I was zealous over the new revelation and was running from anything that looked like the old church structure. I started catching the apostolic in light of this triangle.

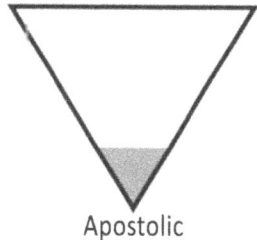
Apostolic

> Now, therefore, you are no longer strangers and foreigners, but fellow citizens with the saints and members of the household of God, having been built on the foundation of the apostles and prophets, Jesus Christ Himself being the chief cornerstone, in whom the whole building, being fitted together, grows into a holy temple in the Lord, in whom you also are being built together for a dwelling place of God in the Spirit (Ephesians 2:19–22).

I love this verse: YOU ARE citizens of the kingdom, the household of God where the foundation is built upon the apostles and prophets and Jesus Christ is the chief cornerstone; and the last part is key—in the Spirit.

Through my experiences in the apostolic house church movement, I have come to embrace the fact that God is absolutely flowing in the house church movement. I believe that the revival God has mandated

Church Fathers vs Kingdom Sons

for this nation and the world will not thrive or be successful without the house church movement blending with the kingdom message. The key is the unity to blend both systems.

During this time with Apostle Brad, I had a wise, elderly gentleman in Buffalo pull me aside one afternoon. He said, "Son, I know this apostle you're talking about. I want to give you a piece of advice and a warning. You're a businessman, and I have watched and observed. When you can no longer pay and be a benefit to him, you will be discarded." I tucked this information in the back of my mind.

The Function of the Apostle

We started building a house church network in Florida and used our relationships and influence to build a prophetic team to provide deliverance and sponsor mini conferences. We provided permanent housing for Apostle Brad and his wife and support while traveling to conferences, deliverance sessions, and building the network.

The office of the apostle is a foundational gift. When it is applied properly, the apostle elevates people from below, pushing others up into their gifts and callings, and releases an individual to be all that God has called him or her to be. There's still an authority structure, but the position is at the lowest point pushing upward for the betterment of individuals. That all sounds good in theory, but there still has to be submission to authority.

Our small group had property in New York that was going to be a pastors' retreat where all the hurt and broken pastors from the old church system could come and get healed.

I can remember Apostle Brad telling me that he would not be a spiritual father to me. We talked about it, and he said there was no way that he could do it; I wondered why. As I look back now, I can tell you. He was a spiritual orphan himself and had his own father issues, which he had carried for many years. His father is in the ministry, and he had some of the same hurts, wounds, and complaints that I did.

Round 8: What Do You Do When Your Reality Check Bounces?

Apostle Brad believed his calling was to grab as many people as he could and help them escape the church system. We had no problem with going into the church system and blowing it up because it was for the better good and God was done with the church system. "This is not what I believe." I am to help the church turn to the kingdom and become the glorious bride.

Deliverance Ministry Lessons

This season was some of the best training I ever had. We performed over 130 deliverances in three days at one conference alone. We assembled six teams of four people, each facilitating deliverances, one right after another. People were being set free and finding God in many different dimensions. I still run into people today who are walking in freedom after all these years. The principles I learned were lifegiving. But there are beliefs that I have had to adjust over time.

Too many times people assumed that in a prophetic deliverance ministry, every strong woman had to be a Jezebel and every weak man was stereotyped as an Ahab. I do believe those spirits exist; and yes, where you're wounded, the enemy will come and exploit those areas. But not every strong woman is a Jezebel, nor is every weak man an Ahab.

This particular area came very close to damaging my relationship with Susie. Did my wife need healing? Absolutely! Because of my all-encompassing devotion to leadership, I could have easily jeopardized my own family since I was taking time away from them to heal others.

This is a warning: The Lord Jesus Christ is your covering, and to Him you must pledge your allegiance. Yes, I understand that the husband covers his wife, but not at the expense of allowing either partner's destiny to be derailed. When I came into Sonship, I understood that the covering was taken care of by Father God, and then it was protection by relationship, not a covering that limited my ability to reach my full potential. When I stand before the Lord Jesus Christ, He will ask me this question: "Where are the wife and children I put you in charge of?"

Small groups are where genuine healing really comes. To quote James 5:16: "Confess your trespasses one to another and pray for one another that you may be healed." In the house church movement, this is done very well due the continuing fellowship and relationship of the participants.

I can remember our criticisms of people in the church system who called themselves apostles. We would say, "They're not apostles, they are pastors on steroids," thinking that we had the new revelation and they didn't.

Agreeing with a Demon

During this time, Susie and I were having a crisis with our son Jason, who had graduated with a 4.0 average from Trinity Christian Academy: a very smart kid! Jason was experimenting with drugs; he loved to smoke pot and get high. As the kids have gotten older, he told us that he used to smoke pot almost every single day before he went to school.

For many years, I'd begged the Lord to help me as a father to bring deliverance and healing to him. One night when Jason was sixteen, at about 3:00 a.m., the Lord showed me prophetically where he hid his drugs. He told me to wake him up, expose his drugs, put them on the counter, and do a Bible teaching on mercy, and then demonstrate mercy by flushing them and never mentioning it again.

I can remember asking the Lord to judge Jason. See, I knew that he needed an encounter with the living God to break his addiction. I personally was pleading with God to judge him as God had judged me. When Jesus walked through the wall to me that night, He told me that if I did not choose Him, He would let hell have its way with me. That was judgment. It was judgment with mercy, because He knew that I was going to choose Him. It was not judgment of wrath ... I was certain God could do it and get through to Jason, but I wasn't sure that I could have that night. After all these years of dealing with the addictions in my life and my family, I had become religious, judgmental, and hard-hearted. In

Round 8: What Do You Do When Your Reality Check Bounces?

some ways, I had become just like my father, standing on my principles with an iron fist.

In spite of the drug use, Jason was a model son. He never broke curfew. He never skipped school, kept perfect grades, was respectful, loved sports, worked hard, and was by all accounts a great kid. He even told me one time that some of his friends asked why he always had money. He told them that he tithed, and therefore God took care of him financially. At first, you might want to say, "That's bogus." But you know, kingdom principles work for the just and the unjust.

Jason graduated from high school and went to a junior college in northern Florida. I can hear him now: "Finally out from underneath the control of Mom and Dad. I can do what I want." Jason had a scholarship playing baseball and was writing for the school paper, but he started doing crack cocaine. It wasn't too long before we knew that he was in trouble. There was only one thing we could do, and that was to pray.

For months, I had a demon spirit visit me every morning and tell me that Jason was going to die because of his drug use. Day after day after day, this spirit would torment me. I became convinced he would die.

But one morning during prayer, my King broke through the noise of that tormenting spirit with a thundering voice: "Now that you have come into agreement with a demon that Jason will die, are you at least man enough to preach his funeral and get his friends saved?"

What a question! The Holy Spirit started to show me how I had come into agreement with this demonic spirit. With that revelation, I broke my covenant and agreement that Jason was going to die and I started to believe the promises that He had given me many years ago. Then the Holy Spirit armed me with the Scripture that I have used to restore both of my sons at points of crisis in their lives:

> I have been young, and now am old; Yet I have not seen the righteous forsaken, Nor his seed begging for bread (Psalm 37:25 KJV).

The Bread of God's Presence

Armed with this Scripture and the knowledge that God is a generational God, I started to do warfare on behalf of my children and the godly lineage that I was supposed to leave. I may still have been an orphan, but I had finally come to the revelation that I was righteous! My being blessed with righteousness doesn't allow my children the right to live a lifestyle that will put them into a place of a beggar. Not a beggar in the natural for bread or in the spiritual for God's presence.

All through Scripture, bread is symbolic of God's presence.

I like the reference of the showbread in the Old Testament, which was behind the veil in the Holy Place. In his book *The God Chasers*, Tommy Tenney taught me to call it the "show up bread." Any time you lean your heart toward His presence, the bread of His presence shows up.

In the book of Ruth, Elimelech and his wife, Naomi, were natives of Bethlehem, which means "House of Bread." There was a famine there, so they traveled to the land of Moab searching for sustenance. My sons and thousands like them are leaving, or have left, the church system for the same reason: "no Bread of His presence." But Moab is a cruel place; it can rob you of your spouse, and you might even bury your sons and daughters and your dreams before their time.

So, when I pray Psalm 37:25 (AMP)—"I have been young and now am old, yet have I not seen the [uncompromisingly] righteous forsaken or their seed begging bread"—I decree that they will not lack His presence, no matter where they need to find it. When Naomi was at her lowest point, still in Moab, she heard a rumor that there was bread back in Bethlehem.

> Then she arose with her daughters-in-law that she might return from the country of Moab, for she had heard in the country of Moab that the Lord had visited His people by giving them bread (Ruth 1:6).

Round 8: What Do You Do When Your Reality Check Bounces?

Moab does what he is allowed to do with our children, but since the devil is on a short leash, their God-given destiny can be preserved through His presence. When our children hunger for the real Bread, they can find it. But most of us don't have His presence, and we can't give what we don't have.

Let's look at the prodigal son story in Luke 15, when the son got so hungry that he came to his senses. He didn't go to the church; he went to his father. But it wasn't the father's love for him, or the robe, ring, or sandals, that restored his identity—it was the celebration.

> You will show me the path of life; In Your presence is fullness of joy; At Your right hand are pleasures forevermore (Psalm 16:11).

> Let my vindications come from Your presence; Let Your eyes look on the things that are upright (Psalm 17:2).

Look what decreeing bread back into their lives brings: joy and vindication from the presence of God. A party, not some hellfire-and-brimstone Bible-thumping mad parent. Our young people crave a party of God's presence, so wherever your child finds bread, go have a party with him and stop preaching to him.

As a mother with a child on crack, Susie was having her own crisis. She would tell me, "If you had not been so religious and dogmatic in your belief system, Jason would not have run to drugs." In some ways, she was probably right. Jason went to school at Trinity Christian Academy, which was part of the church, and saw all the corruption; in reality, he had plenty of natural excuses to resist God.

I remember that in the middle of a heated argument with Susie, I yelled back at her, "I might be a Jesus freak, but Jesus promised me my family. Jesus promised to restore my marriage and my sons. And I'm standing on that promise."

I can tell you that all hell will try to stop you from believing the promises that only God can pull off.

As for Me and My House...

Months later, I attended a Promise Keepers meeting in Tampa. In the midst of 40,000 men, we were worshiping to "As For Me and My House, We Will Serve the Lord." I broke down and started crying. I asked the Lord if I had sinned and canceled God's ability to give me the promise of my son and family. My son was doing crack and my wife was battling depression. I couldn't sing the song "As for Me and My House, We Will Serve the Lord" because my home was fractured and my house was broken.

The Lord assured me that I had been faithful. And then He spoke. "Charlie, most of the men in this stadium do not know what it would cost them to be faithful to me. But you have been faithful. Go home and tell Susie to prepare the fatted calf. And tell her Jason will not die."

For years I'd asked God to judge Jason so he could break his addiction, and the Lord said to me, "Charlie, I'm going to judge Jason."

If Jesus took the sins of the world unto Himself, then the world no longer has a sin problem. It only has a revelation problem of who Jesus is and what He did on the cross.

Since I had asked God to do this for years, you would've thought my response would be, "It's about time!" Instead, I started begging God to show him mercy! When God judges His children, His judgment is always laced with mercy to draw us back to Him. There is a day allocated for the final judgment; I personally believe that day has already come and gone, that it was the day they crucified Jesus. If Jesus took the sins of the world unto Himself, then the world no longer has a sin problem.

Round 8: What Do You Do When Your Reality Check Bounces?

It only has a revelation problem of who Jesus is and what He did on the cross. If I am wrong and there is another day, then I am still covered. Until then, I will try to walk in love and power. I am not looking to be raptured from earth; I am personally looking to take over earth as I bring heaven here daily. The problem is you can't bring heaven to earth if you don't go to heaven!

The Son Comes Home

I had a preacher who asked me if I believed in the rapture, and I said, "Why, yes I do. I go to heaven at least three or four times a day." He didn't think that was funny because he won't die to himself and is waiting to escape instead of taking over.

> **Kingdom Key: Many times your best indicator of success is your enemies and not your friends.**

I figured out how to tell Susie what God had said. The questions came running through our heads.

"What does 'He won't die mean'?"

"Susie, it means God is getting ready to do something and he won't die. Don't have any other answers; just believe."

Ten days later, Jason had come from northern Florida down to the Daytona Beach area to party with some of his old friends. At four o'clock in the morning, there was a knock on the front door. His friend Brad was panicked: "Mr. Coker, Jason's in the front seat of the car, and he has passed out. He hasn't slept in days and he's lost his mind. He has overdosed. The last coherent thing he told us to do was, 'Get me to my Daddy. He'll know what to do.'"

Church Fathers vs Kingdom Sons

We brought him into the house. I laid him on the couch with his head in my lap, and I started praying in the Spirit. Susie was telling me to take him to the hospital. "No, God said he would not die!" At nine o'clock the next morning, Jason and I got on our knees and completely surrendered our lives to the Lord Jesus Christ for the use of the kingdom. We had a small deliverance time. Before I left the house to go to work, I walked into the bedroom, and my wife was in bed with the covers pulled over her head, trying to surrender to her depression.

As I sat on the bed, I spoke firmly, yet lovingly. "Susie, God didn't take us this far to abandon us now. God has a plan. So get out of this bed, get your Bible out, do your devotions, figure out what that plan is, and do your part."

As I was opening the store, the phone rang, and it was Susie. "You're not to believe what my devotion was today," she told me. "I opened my devotional, and the heading was 'God has a plan.'"

Jason returned to college. A couple weeks later, he called me. "Dad, I had one of your crazy visions. In this vision God showed me how He's always had His hand on my baseball, and He's going to take me to Division One college ball. Dad, God says He's going to pay for my school. God wants to use my baseball skills and has a purpose for my life."

It was great news that God was starting to speak to my son in visions about a given purpose, especially the part where God said He was going to pay for it, because I had cut Jason off because of his drug abuse. But God does have a plan, and luckily this wasn't going to cost me a cent!

Jason's friend Matt, who had brought him to the house that night, was playing baseball at Bethune-Cookman University in Daytona Beach. Jason himself wound up earning a scholarship to play baseball at the historically black college. (Sure glad I dealt with my racism!)

Several weeks later, I was in prayer at about three o'clock in the morning. The Lord asked me if I was willing to relinquish my

Round 8: What Do You Do When Your Reality Check Bounces?

responsibility as a father over Jason. I saw the position of authority, anointing, and the generational aspect of fathering, and now He was asking me to lay it on the altar for a season. He said that if I was willing to relinquish this position, He would bring another man into his life who would father him for a season and bring some healing to his wounds. And when this season was over, He would hand him back to me.

Little did I know that Jason was walking by the science building and saw an inscription that read "All science points to God." He felt like the Lord told him to change his degree from business to religion and philosophy. As he walked into the religion and philosophy building, he ran into the department head, Dr. James Brooks. Later, when Dr. Brooks and I compared notes, the encounter was about the same time God was asking me if I was willing to relinquish my rights as a father. God was telling this educated black professor to treat Jason as a son. God used Dr. Brooks to bring the necessary healing to Jason that I could not. Jason played baseball and became the director of the fellowship of Christian athletes.

Jason finished his four years of college and earned a degree in religion and philosophy. Thanks to Dr. Brooks' influence, he proceeded to attend Oral Roberts University and earned a master's degree in biblical literature.

My willingness to let another man father my son in the areas of my weakness came back to me full circle in business when Jason fathered me for a season and ran the business instead of me.

The Bastard Curse

After Jason got married and graduated from Oral Roberts University, he moved back to the area. We set up a deliverance session for him and his wife. Since he was my son, I was asked not to be on the team; I simply sat in the next room and interceded for them both. As Apostle Brad led the deliverance session, the rest of the team could not catch the curse that was on Jason. Apostle Brad asked Jason for my help because he wanted an outside confirmation of the vision God showed him.

To my surprise, when he asked me what curse was on Jason, I blurted out, "A 'bastard curse'!" The vision God had showed him was of my mother-in-law walking up to Jason when he was born in the hospital, grabbing his little toes, and saying, "You're a bastard." At that spoken word, a demon was assigned to Jason to fulfill that curse. This didn't seem fair. I married his mother, and I became his father. The bottom line was, Jason was conceived outside of a marriage covenant. Even though eventually we did what was right, I did not deal with that curse at the time. The curse was upon my son from the day he was conceived.

> A bastard shall not enter into the congregation of the Lord; even to his tenth generation shall he not enter into the congregation of the Lord (Deuteronomy 23:2 KJV).

Once this curse was broken, Jason and I became best friends. Doors opened for us to do business and ministry together. And for the first time, with this curse broken, we started to become family at a heart level.

The blood of Jesus and the cross cancel the curse, but we have to enforce the power of the blood to redeem our inheritance.

I've told this story and have had altar calls as I travel and preach. I'm totally shocked by how many people come to have this curse broken off of them. I've seen grandmas bring children up. I've seen as much as 50 percent of a congregation come to the altar. The blood of Jesus and the cross cancel the curse, but we have to enforce the power of the blood to redeem our inheritance.

An apostle who works from the foundation of the pyramid and lifts people up spiritually is truly how this model needs to function. Let me

Round 8: What Do You Do When Your Reality Check Bounces?

show you. When people see a beautiful mansion, they gush over the furniture, the lovely columns, the walls and windows, yet few even notice the foundation. The structure needed to support the mansion and everything in it is usually covered by dirt. How was it even possible to build the foundation in rocky soil? Of course, dynamite was used to blow out the boulders and root systems to make the foundation as strong as could be. I believe that's the purpose of the deliverance ministry: to dig down deep into the lives of God's people and blow out the rocks, roots, and generational sins. With these things removed, there's a foundation to build something unbreakable that symbolizes the kingdom—an absolute necessity for true kingdom life!

The Dreadful Call

During this time, one of my spiritual sons, who had worked for me and been under my wing for years, went to work for a very large ministry in Orlando. Through his relationships with the ministry, he formed a company that generated tremendous income from people who were supporting many ministries. To make a long story short, we started working together and for several years poured tens of thousands of dollars back into ministry. I had become the anointed businessman who brought finances to the ministry. "Now this was the wealth of the wicked stored up for the righteous."

If you've ever seen *Deadliest Catch* on the Discovery Channel, it's easy to understand. When the guys are catching pots full of crab, the captain is a hero; but once the pots start pulling up empty, everyone's out for the captain's head.

Needless to say, what we thought was the Holy Ghost gravy train was about to come to a screeching halt. I went from being a Joseph in Potiphar's house to a demonic security breach in one phone call.

On a trip to New York, while hanging out with Apostle Brad, I told him that I believed the Lord had shown me that I was one of the keys to revival in America. I had visions about the coming move of

Church Fathers vs Kingdom Sons

God; I'd seen my mother's prayers, and a vision had shown my mother walking up the hill praying about the end-time harvests and envisioning the glory cloud of God saving, healing, and delivering, all at the same time. His presence left an imprint on my spirit that still drives me to His presence today.

As I shared the intimate details of what I believed the Lord had shown me, I did not know that Apostle Brad believed I was arrogant even as I was speaking the words.

The next day, the phone rang with dreadful news: a call that no one ever wants. My business partner was on the line: "The FBI has come to the office and seized all of our assets. You need to get on a plane and come home!"

That night, I rented a room at the Hampton Inn in Rochester, New York, waiting for a flight out in the morning. My mind was spinning: "What had gone wrong? Had this truly been a Ponzi scheme? Oh God, I have to face all of our investors!" I asked if this was God. "God, I have my life savings in this! God, we have $5.1 million! God, am I going to jail? God, You know my heart!"

When I get into a situation where I need to really hear God and can't get alone in the woods or in my car, I love to take long, hot showers. So I took a long, hot shower in my room at the hotel. I didn't know what I was going to face the next day with the FBI. Things were so out of my control that I stayed in the shower too long and my body started to overheat.

I can remember this as if it were yesterday. A spirit of suicide came into that bathroom and spoke to me. It hissed, "If you'll stay in the shower just a little longer, when they find your body they will think it was an accident." I had battled the spirit of suicide earlier in my life, but that voice had come from the inside. This time, I heard it from the outside; recognizing that, I looked at this spirit and answered back, "It's only a few million dollars and my reputation. What's the big deal?"

Round 8: What Do You Do When Your Reality Check Bounces?

That visitation with the spirit of suicide actually empowered me to know that God had a bigger plan for me. I knew that the devil is the father of lies and was trying to get me to take myself out so I wouldn't be in position to plunder the kingdom of darkness.

The devil tried to push my buttons: "What if you go to jail?" I told the devil that Paul wrote some of his best books of the Bible from jail, and I knew that God had told me I would write books one day.

I begged God for the strength to man up and face the music. I realized that we HAD been involved in a $160 million Ponzi scheme.

We lost all our finances and assets … seemingly everything. This was probably the most critical emotional crisis that we had faced as a family in ten years. With one phone call, my reputation was gone and my company was in jeopardy. I feared going to jail. It was overwhelming.

I can tell you that my heart was pure, but the people we were connected to were wrong. My intentions were to financially support ministry, and we did. The Kingdom Key I learned was: **"You can lose your reputation and still have your integrity."**

You can lose your reputation and still have your integrity.

In the midst of this, I felt word curses coming from people I trusted. They weren't just words from investors and friends who had been hurt and confused by all this, but a demonic assault in these curses from a hidden source. So one night I prayed, "Lord, I need to figure out how to battle this and where it's coming from."

I went into a prophetic vision in which I went back in time, into the dining room of Apostle Brad during Thanksgiving dinner. Because of the call about the FBI, I had flown home the day before. I listened as Tim told everyone who was there, including people with whom I had been connected spiritually and raised up, that I had become a security breach due to my arrogance and pride in thinking that I was a key to revival. God exposed the word curses to me from that evening!

Finally Forgiveness

After this prophetic encounter, I started asking the Lord what was going on. Only a major crisis like that could force me to open my eyes and get me to leave the apostolic system, and it sure was major! It felt as if the apostolic ministry that I believed would usher in this great end-time harvest was turning on me.

I carried the information from the prophetic encounter for over three months and shared it with no one. One day I got Apostle Brad in my vehicle and pulled off on a dirt road. (I wanted to shoot him, but King Jesus wouldn't let me.) I told him about the encounter I had had and what God had shown me. He started tearing up and asking me to forgive him! He appeared to be totally astonished. God had just given him the revelation, as we spoke, that I was petrified to stand in the pulpit and preach. His assumption that I was arrogant and prideful was wrong. I was simply too afraid and insecure to move into another realm of gifting.

Needless to say, I was battling major depression and hopelessness since everything I had worked for was gone. I jeopardized my entire family and my company; my ministry reputation was toast; and yeah, I went into a deep depression. Most people assumed my depression was because of the financial losses. I do have to admit it definitely had a part to play, but my biggest sadness was that I had put my whole heart into the apostolic system. I truly believed I would be doing ministry with these people until the day I met Jesus face-to-face. (I'm one of those "all-in" guys). When we don't know who we are as sons, we battle fears and insecurities and cover them with arrogance and pride. Depending upon a prophetic word or vision to hear from God and keeping it to yourself allows others to misread and often judge you. Sad to say, the relationship between Apostle Brad and I never recovered.

Round 8: What Do You Do When Your Reality Check Bounces?

A Time of Healing

God sent me to a church in Daytona while I was still building ministry in the house church movement with Apostle Brad. Pastor Scott** leads this church and is an apostle; his wife, Karen, is a prophet. They're connected with Bishop Bill Hamon. I saw the apostolic and prophetic work hand in hand. The first time that I went to one of their meetings, the Lord gave me a word to release to the church. Unsure, I told the Lord that if He wanted me to release the word, He needed to speak to the authority in the house. Pastor Karen prophetically called me out and said, "God told you to give a word. Why didn't you release it?" So, I went forward and gave the word. The following week, I returned, and the same thing happened. She rebuked me again for not releasing the word God had given me. It became obvious between us that they knew who I was by the Spirit, and we started building a relationship.

For a year or so, I was part of this church and observed how the apostle and prophet worked together. I saw traces of the old wineskins being the church system, but also saw the apostolic working as foundational triangle downward. This was a great time of healing for me; I was received as a prophet and released to do ministry, and I thrived in the environment.

Apostle Scott called me to the office one day; and on the ride over there, I said to Susie, "I have been to these kinds of meetings before, so I'm not sure what to expect today." But to my surprise what I saw was truly triangle-down, pushing-up fathering.

Apostle Scott and Karen asked me how I was doing, told me I had been at the church for over a year, and asked if I felt healed and ready to do what I was called to do. He let me know that he recognized that I was not simply a house prophet, and he wanted me to start traveling again. I needed to stop hanging around the church; when I showed up, I brought unrest to what he was trying to accomplish. The regional gifting was not being used properly and I was bringing unrest to the whole house. He said to check in and give testimony, but to begin to travel again and fulfill my destiny.

Church Fathers vs Kingdom Sons

This was a breath of fresh air. I wasn't asked to leave: I was told to go do what I was called to do.

When I stand before the Lord Jesus Christ, He will ask me this question: "Where are the wife and children I put you in charge of?" They are doing great!

***

Kingdom Keys:

1. You can lose your reputation and still have integrity.
2. If you cannot love by your standards, you cannot live by them either.
3. Remember the cross and the blood of Jesus cancels all curses.
4. All hell will try to stop you from believing the promises that only God can pull off. Stand firm in His promises always.
5. Many times, your best indicator of success is your enemies and not your friends.

Round 9

Who's in Charge: Father? Or Son?

About the time you think you have a handle on the revelation that the Lord has given you, He has a habit of testing you to see if you're willing to obey those principles.

I remember the phone calls I received from my son Jason, who was living in Tulsa, Oklahoma, and finishing his degree in biblical literature. The phone calls often went something like this: "Dad, the Lord has revealed to me that I'm supposed to come and work for you." Usually I would fire back, "Jason, it's not God. You have a degree in Bible, and now you're going to sell lighting and light bulbs for me? No." Click.

Ring, ring: "Dad, listen to me. God has told me that I'm supposed to move home and work for you at the store." "Jason, I don't believe it's God. You have a degree in Bible, and you wanted to further your education." Click!

Ring, ring: "Dad, don't hang up on me. Listen to me! I *know* it's God, and I *am* coming to go to work for you. You need me, and I'm coming to do that."

"Jason, are you sure this is God? If it is, we'll work out the details."

I can hear you asking, "Why would a father make it so difficult for a son to tell him what God had shown him?" I did that because I knew that working for me would be very difficult. If he wasn't 100 percent sure it was God, there would not be grace enough for him to survive. I did it because when it got tough and he wanted to quit, he would know God had sent him. I can't tell you the hell that we went through, learning the process of the apostolic downward triangle, or the idiosyncrasies of running the family business, which was in financial difficulty, especially with three strong personalities.

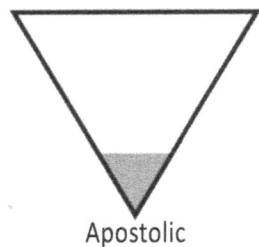

Apostolic

Too Many Hats

I already had a manager when Jason came to the store to work, so for two years Jason had to submit to both the manager and me.

It's difficult running a family business at times. There are so many different hats to wear: you don't know if you are wearing the hat of the business owner, father, boss, or husband because your wife is hanging around too and keeping the books. (And if Momma ain't happy, no one is.)

I can remember one day when Susie and I got into an argument at the store about something she had done. Man, did we get into a fight! The whole place knew that we were fighting. The next morning, my manager shrugged and asked, "Dude, I know God healed your marriage, but after yesterday's fight, my question is why?"

I said, "That's a loaded question from somebody who almost lost his marriage because his communication skills were so poor, he couldn't tell his wife how he really felt." My manager just had a deer-in-headlights expression. "Listen, Susie and I believe in the

Round 9: Who's in Charge: Father? Or Son?

kingdom principle, 'Don't let the sun go down on your wrath.' We fixed it before we went to bed, and actually were romantic."

Years ago, a Christian counselor told me my marriage would never succeed, but we're still here. So, I have a hard time hearing advice from people who have been divorced three or four times. I am teachable, and I definitely need help. I don't know many people who have restored a broken marriage like ours. (Susie and I will explain in detail in *From Rape to Righteousness: Redeeming the Bride of Christ*.)

After a couple of years, Jason came to me and said he had made a decision. He wanted a place within the company. So he sat me down and laid out a business plan. As I was reviewing his business plan and his proposals, the Holy Spirit started speaking to me about this apostolic triangle being the foundation. I believe that the apostolic carries the fathering mantle for the kingdom. The Lord started speaking to me about giving Jason complete control over the company. He said that Jason was a much better businessman than I was. I'm a great salesman; that's my strength in business. My own orphan spirit and insecurities only emphasized my weaknesses. I've needed someone to cover those weaknesses, so I've always had partners. I gave up a lot of my authority to the other people instead of leading as I was called to do and allowing others to fill the weak places.

The Lord asked me to give Jason complete control over the company. He was to have all the assets at his disposal to run it as he saw fit. I had been my own boss for over twenty-five years. Susie and I had weathered multiple storms, and we had always come out on top. It was us against the world, and God was asking me to give control to a twenty-four-year-old. It sure was a big blow to my ego! I didn't know God was trying to teach me how the apostolic was supposed to work in real life and not just in theory.

Church Fathers vs Kingdom Sons

If you look at Scripture, you'll find that Jesus did not start performing miracles, which expanded the kingdom, until God the Father audibly spoke a blessing for all to hear:

> When all the people were baptized, it came to pass that Jesus also was baptized; and while He prayed, the heaven was opened. And the Holy Spirit descended in bodily form like a dove upon Him, and a voice came from heaven which said, "You are My beloved Son; in You I am well pleased" (Luke 3:21–22).

Learning to Give the Father's Blessing

The Lord was teaching me the power of a father's blessing, which releases the true identity into the son. God was showing me to empower Jason with my blessing, sending the message that if you do business with Jason, you are doing business with me.

According to tradition, that's what a Jewish father would do in the middle of the town square. He would present his son, who was his apprentice in training, and publicly declare his approval of his son. In doing so, he was telling the town that "from now on, if you do business with him, you are also doing business with me. He has full authority to do the family business."

When Jesus was twelve and got in trouble for staying behind in Jerusalem and talking to the leaders in the temple, He tried to explain to Mary that He had been granted the Father's authority but did not have the maturity of favor from man. He was still under the authority of his parents. When we begin to come into our true understanding of God the Father, and our Sonship to Him is revealed, He will also anoint us to do business on His behalf by the power of His blessing. First Peter 3:9 puts it this way: "Not returning evil for evil or reviling for reviling, but on the contrary blessing, knowing that you were called to this, that you may inherit a blessing."

Round 9: Who's in Charge: Father? Or Son?

Blessings have tremendous power to cancel evil. Position yourself to inherit a blessing! God's blessing on you is much greater than the public validation of a father toward his son.

One of the first hurdles we had to overcome was when Jason decided to fire his brother Bryan. This was made a little easier because the day he fired Bryan, I had asked an electrician friend of mine if he would hire Bryan. So Jason fired him and gave him a job at the same time.

The next decision was a little more difficult. Jason said to me, "Dad, you and Mom have made a living, but this is a mom-and-pop shop. If we are ever going to be a real company, we have to fire Mom." Jason knew we needed different skills than my wife possessed, but telling her was the scariest thing we had ever had to do. (I told Jason that he had to do it because I close both eyes when I sleep!) You have to remember, Susie was the warehouse girl when the employees were sick, and she worked nights if necessary. She filled any gap.

When we presented it to her at first, she was a little upset. She felt as if we were pushing her out of the company. What we were really doing was giving control over to Jason, so he could manage differently. As it worked out, she continued to work at the company. Jason took control of paying the bills and setting budgets, and she worked beside him. Truth be known, he took most of the pressure that she'd been carrying from her. Once Jason made a decision, it was his way or the highway. I sure was glad it worked out: I have to live with her!

Several years earlier, I had been complaining to the Lord about Susie. I was telling God I didn't think she was spiritual enough. The Lord told me to go ask her about the condition of her store checkbook. When I did, she asked me to come into agreement with her in prayer to believe that God would bring her in $5,000 by Friday to pay the current bills. So we prayed. As I left the office that

Church Fathers vs Kingdom Sons

day, the Lord let me know: "Susie is using her faith to bring in the finances for this company to survive. Do not question her spiritual condition by your gifting. Your ways are not always My ways. You need to be more sensitive with her. She was My daughter before she was your wife."

A few years later, after Jason and I had rapidly opened new branches, I complained about Susie's spiritual condition again. The Lord spoke to me: "Go ask her about the condition of the company checkbook." When I did, she said, "It's not a big deal. I'm just believing God to bring in $96,000 by Friday, so I can cover these checks that I have written." I guess her faith had grown!

Running a business with kingdom principles is a difficult thing to do with several strong personalities. I was challenged because God had put Jason in control. I had to be sure that I was hearing God when I spoke and then be patient, giving others time to respond or not. This was a very difficult lesson for me. There was a carpet store next door, and we shared a warehouse. One day they overheard Jason and me arguing. (The TV show *Orange County Choppers*, in which Paul Sr. and Paul Jr. yell, scream, cuss, and throw things, was a pretty good representation of our arguments, without the cussing … sometimes.) The carpet store folks started screaming back, "Hey Pauly," and mocking us like the TV show.

Honoring the Gifting of Others Takes Love and Patience

I went to the Lord and asked how we could communicate and make this work. He said to me, "The issue is your lack of honor of his gifting. If you will honor his gifting, he will in turn honor yours. Then you will be on the same page." One of the kingdom principles that God has taught me is, "You cannot have what you don't honor." The following picture was hung in an office that Jason and I shared. When you looked at my desk and then his, it made sense. Just remember, the boats got tied up on both sides of the dock.

Round 9: Who's in Charge: Father? Or Son?

About this time, I was working mostly in the office where my spiritual son and I were doing the joint-venture business, not at the lighting store. But when that Ponzi scheme blew up in my face, the whole family and the business were put into a major crisis. With the crisis at hand, Jason cut my salary in half, fired half of our staff, and made the company lean and mean, so we could become profitable quickly.

Jason had become totally focused on money and the condition of the company. Under that stress, he lacked sensitivity in the area of my personal finances and had become what Susie called "Mr. Pissy Pants."

One day I was about to let him have it, and the Lord said, "He is your authority. Submit to him with the right attitude, and I will give you favor with your boss." I have to tell you that was a little hard to take. Technically, I owned the whole company; I was this kid's father; and I believed I could kick his butt.

The Lord said I was only right on one of the three counts. Number one, the Lord said He owned the company because I had given it to Him. Number two, I was Jason's father. Number three, Jason would probably win in a fistfight. So the Lord said to me, "Why don't you sit down and speak to him like a father and not a disgruntled employee? If you have any complaints, remember: you raised this boy."

Under Jason's leadership, we started functioning as a well-oiled machine. God would give me a vision or speak to me in a word. I would present it to Jason. He would then process it totally differently than I did. But, every time, we would come to the same conclusion: the Lord was telling us to expand or make major business decisions. When I honored his gifting and gave him time and space, he would always come to the conclusion that I already had. The great part about Jason was that he not only came to the same conclusion, he came with a blueprint on how to execute it.

During this season I learned how to communicate with Jason and teach him people skills that he sorely lacked. He was a black-and-white, nuts-and-bolts, by-the-numbers administrator. So I fathered him over coffee, on a drive to one of our branches, or on different projects that we worked on together. Jason allowed me to father him in the area of his people skills. This was the most fruitful season of my life with my son. He'd become my best friend and my business partner, and he took care of my administrative issues for the ministry.

God has shown me the blueprint of the apostolic of the church. A spiritual father, still in his prime, gives control to his son, gets underneath, and pushes him to the top.

I can remember manufacturers' reps with whom I had done business for twenty years coming to me and saying, "Hey, Jason is no longer buying my product." I would tell them that Jason had made the decision because their pricing was not right, or they didn't have the right product. They would say to me, "Aren't you the owner? Don't you make these decisions? We've done business for twenty years." I had to tell them, "I may be the owner on paper, but Jason is the boss. If Jason says no, it's no. You haven't earned his business."

Jason became the golden boy in our industry because our company began to thrive under his leadership. One of the old-time reps came back

Round 9: Who's in Charge: Father? Or Son?

from the Dallas market with a story that I've pondered in my heart for years. A bunch of businesspeople were talking about our company and how Jason had turned the company around. They were bragging about how competent Jason was and his good business decisions, and rightly so. But this old rep said something interesting. He said, "You know, I've been around a bit longer than some of you guys. I can remember when Charlie Coker was on the back stoop of his business, praying that God would deliver that boy from drugs. Charlie told me that one day God was going to deliver him and he would be in business and ministry with him." One of the other reps at the table, who knew me very well, made a joke and said, "Charlie surely does pray a lot. I tried to pray the other morning, but God put me on hold and told me He was on the phone with Charlie. I'd have to wait."

The Modern-Day Apostle

As I'm writing this chapter, I'm thinking about all of the principles of the kingdom the Lord has taught me through my business and all the people that I have affected.

> **One of the reasons why the church is so weak is because we've elevated the priesthood and devalued the businessman and his spiritual effectiveness within our communities.**

What I've learned about businessmen is that they are kings. When you look at Scripture, you see that the king went, did business, and brought resources for the priest to do his job. I believe the church system has a tendency to rate the businessman for his finances and not for his spirituality, wisdom, and his entrepreneurial gifting. I see that one of the reasons why the church is so weak is because we've elevated the priesthood and devalued the businessman and his spiritual effectiveness within our communities.

During this season, the Lord had already convinced me that I walked in the office of a prophet, but was telling me that I was also an apostle. He started waking me up at 4:48 every morning until I submitted to that call.

> Then Jesus said to him, "Unless you people see signs and wonders, you will by no means believe" (John 4:48).

> Truly the signs of an apostle were accomplished among you with all perseverance, in signs and wonders and mighty deeds (2 Corinthians 12:12).

I asked the Lord, "If the Scripture is true, what does the function of a modern-day apostle look like?"

So the next morning, He sent me to a coffee shop in town owned by a Christian businessman I knew. As I got my coffee and sat down at the table, the Holy Spirit asked me if I thought I was an apostle. I replied, "You said I was, and therefore I must be." At that point He told me that I carry the government of the kingdom upon my life as an apostle. Wade, the business owner, was in desperate need of $1,000 to pay his coffee bill or he would not be able to do business. (Everybody wants to hear God better, unless it costs them.)

Previously, that wouldn't have been a problem. I would have written a check or used a credit card. Now, however, I was under a mandate to submit all financial giving to Jason and my wife because I have a habit of giving away the farm and then putting God's name on it.

So God had just put me in a corner. What a pickle! I asked the Lord, "As an apostle and a government official of the kingdom, what do I do?" He said to declare and to decree $1,000 to show up in my hands so I could give it to Wade. I started praying under my breath, whispering and decreeing that $1,000 would manifest and show up. Then I could do what I was called to do as a government official of the kingdom. I was on my

Round 9: Who's in Charge: Father? Or Son?

third hour there, my eighth cup of coffee, and getting disgusted with this training program God put me in. I closed my eyes and visualized God the Father handing me $1,000 so I could give it to one of His other sons.

At that point, my friend Roger walked through the door. Roger got his coffee and sat down at my table, and I said to him, "Glad you finally obeyed God and came to bring me my thousand dollars."

Roger asked, "What thousand dollars?"

I looked Roger in the eyes. "Where is my money?"

He started laughing and asked, "How did you know I had this check for you?" Roger had written a check three days earlier for $1,000, made out to my ministry. With that, we called Wade over to the table. I told Wade what God had shown me. I signed the check over to him. He started to weep. He told us that he'd been in the office asking God for the money to pay his coffee bill so he could stay in business.

Learning Kingdom Government

The training that I would need in order to understand how government in the kingdom really works had begun. We need to be able to take responsibility for the sins of the past and have a clear vision of the kingdom of the future in order to have authority in cities, businesses, churches, and regions.

> **We need to be able to take responsibility for the sins of the past and have a clear vision of the kingdom of the future in order to have authority in cities, businesses, churches, and regions.**

I began to get a clearer understanding how God was teaching me through business. I saw that the kingdom functions with heavenly mandates and the blueprints of heaven manifest on earth through His fivefold ministry.

As I look back, I see that the lighting showroom we built in St. Augustine, Florida, near Jacksonville, was a complete stretch of faith at the time. God told us to build a new showroom with a design center. He also said to shift our business plan so we could do more lighting design and not be limited to national builders' accounts. It had been over twenty years since I had done high-end design work. It's like the Lord said, "You build it and they will come."

This particular showroom was twenty miles south of Jacksonville. Two weeks before we were going to open, I met Steve, who had been an owner of one of the largest lighting showrooms in Florida. The high-end design market was his area of expertise. When I met him, I immediately saw the Holy Spirit on his life. I also saw the brokenness. He had recently been driven out of the company that he had built and owned for over thirty years. He was now working out of an office with an electrician just 150 yards from this new showroom. To make a long story short, we became partners. His skills meshed perfectly within our design center.

During our relationship, I had to continue to remind him not to be bitter and angry with his ex-partner and the loss of his company. When his ex-partner's firm went bankrupt, we were able to purchase the name rights and the inventory of his old company.

When you do business with the kingdom in mind, God will use you to help restore to others what was lost—relationally, financially, and spiritually.

I remember the day I had a meltdown in the warehouse, trying to load trucks and salvage the inventory. I was staying in Jacksonville,

Round 9: Who's in Charge: Father? Or Son?

working like a dog eighteen hours a day. I went to the showroom where Steve was meeting with a guy who had money to invest in the rebirth of the old company. He was a believer also, but he was needed because he could write big checks. I felt like a "dirtball" and was very ticked off at the whole situation.

I remember the Lord showing up in the corner of the warehouse. He started to speak to me. He told me that He was very proud that I was willing to do my part in redeeming a brother's inheritance that had been lost. He showed me that the day was coming when I would not only do the labor part but also write the checks to help redeem the sons of God's inheritance.

When Jason and I decided to close the business, Steve and his partner took over that location and then reopened a store in Jacksonville area. When you do business with the kingdom in mind, God will use you to help restore to others what was lost—relationally, financially, and spiritually.

Here's an example of how you know your employees have figured out that you and God have a covenant relationship about business. One day my manager slammed down the phone and said, "If God owns this company, tell Him that He is on credit hold with Value Lighting. They are not sending any more product until He sends them a check!" I remember God telling me I could use my faith or my credit, but that if I continued to use credit, He would get none of the credit that He rightly deserved. He was trying to teach me how to push and make something happen by faith rather than by my own striving.

Kingdom Key: If you always use YOUR credit, God will never get HIS credit.

I can tell you it was very satisfying to do ministry for years. I was going to New York once a month, learning how the kingdom functions, and was able to pay my own way so that if the offering was small it didn't matter. I believe the apostle Paul set the stage for businessmen to function as apostles in the marketplace.

As I was writing this chapter, Tony, one of my former employees, just happened to text me that he "loved me" out of the blue. I don't think that was a coincidence. So I called him and told that I was just explaining how in business, people's lives are impacted to expand the kingdom. He let me know that I had been a great role model for him because I taught him how the prophetic worked. The timing of his message shocked both of us! God is cool!

Returning to New York

God asked me to start traveling back to New York again. I felt like I had taken two different missionary trips: one with the church system (triangle up) and the other with the apostolic house church system (triangle down). I had some success bringing unity between the two. In some cases, the only unity was that they all disagreed with me. aha

I let God know if I went back to New York, I expected to witness power as demonstrated in the book of Acts or I was not wasting my time. He then reminded me of the Rolex watch He had promised as a sign of this revival.

My wife and Jason had given me a Tag Heuer watch worth about $1,600 ... a nice watch, but not a Rolex! As the date was getting closer to travel again, I started to crank up the prayers. As I prayed, the Lord told me to connect with different people, to rebuild old relationships and form new ones.

Could my return to New York be a sign that the Lord was promoting me in the kingdom, since every time there was a promotion in the Spirit it came after some form of death cycle? I had certainly been murdered the last time I was in New York, if you remember! Jesus said it this way in John 12:23–26:

Round 9: Who's in Charge: Father? Or Son?

But Jesus answered them, saying, "The hour has come that the Son of Man should be glorified. Most assuredly, I say to you, unless a grain of wheat falls into the ground and dies, it remains alone; but if it dies, it produces much grain. He who loves his life will lose it, and he who hates his life in this world will keep it for eternal life. If anyone serves Me, let him follow Me; and where I am, there My servant will be also. If anyone serves Me, him My Father will honor."

With Jesus as our example, God tries to put His glory upon us as sons. The process of death, burial, and resurrection is the same for us as it was for Him; but most of the time, we run from every death process that God puts before us and call it demonic. Some of the time, it is actually God trying to kill our flesh and our attitudes.

Many times, taking us from one position of authority to a greater position of authority requires a separation from those with whom we have covenanted. Often, a re-evaluation of the covenants with the people with whom you've walked in the last season is needed. The covenant between you and God is the highest covenant of all. The second covenant is between you and your spouse. Many people have gotten born again, but their covenant was with the church and not the living God. So, when the church crumbles, they crumble with it.

> **Many times, taking us from one position of authority to a greater position of authority requires a separation from those with whom we have covenanted.**

You might think that as I write this that I know what I'm doing, but let me tell you, I haven't had a clue many times and am just now understanding that this is been a journey and a process. Please don't use the last statement as an excuse to walk in rebellion, manipulation, or in the spirit of accusation against the authority figures to whom God has told you to submit. As God kept prompting me to start traveling again to New York, I definitely had an attitude and did not want to deal with the root issues in my heart.

To be honest, I could not have cared less about relationships at this point. All I wanted was revival, in spite of what God wanted. As I kept pushing God, He started to rebuke me for my attitude. He kept telling me that I was pushing Him out of His timing and that I needed to be patient and do ministry His way, in His timing.

One morning, God spoke to me about timing, and He asked if I wanted the Rolex He had promised. "Yes, I sure do! It is a sign for the timing of revival. That's what I've been looking for." He told me to give my Tag to Anthony, one of my employees. I let Susie and Jason know what God told me about giving Anthony my watch. I asked them for permission, because they were my authority in giving. I asked God to confirm the time for me to give Anthony his gift.

The following week, Anthony, Jason, and I were going to the Dallas lighting show. As we were walking down into the airplane, Anthony looked at Jason and me and said, "Wow, I'm going to the lighting show with the bosses! I need to look sharp, and I probably need to buy a new watch." Jason looked at me and said, "Redneck, there's your sign. Give your watch to Anthony." I explained to Anthony what all this meant. I told him about God's promise back in 1996 about giving me a Rolex as the sign of revival coming. He took it with gladness.

Do You Want a Fake Revival?

We spent three nights in Dallas and arrived home late that Saturday night. I woke up early Sunday morning and started off my prayers with my demand list. I was telling God what I expected the next weekend in New York. God interrupted me abruptly, and He was not very happy with me. He yelled at me and asked, "Who do you think you're talking to?"

Round 9: Who's in Charge: Father? Or Son?

At that point, I knew I had entered into the dead man's zone with God. He informed me that He did not want to hear my prayers any longer. He reminded me of a black pastor, Ricky, who had a church in Sanford, Florida. I had been in several meetings with him in the last few months, and man, could he pray! He would pray, and the atmosphere changed.

God then gave me very clear instructions. I was to go by the office, get a company check for $300, go find Ricky's church that morning, and give him my prayer list. He didn't want to hear me speak to Him any longer. He was ticked off. I did as I was told. I looked in the phone book, found Ricky's church in Sanford, and drove about thirty minutes to go attend his church service.

As I came into the building, Pastor Ricky recognized me and was honored that I would come. He handed me the microphone and asked me to share with the people. I told them I had gotten in trouble with God that morning because I had treated Him like a waiter and that He had told me to bring a check for $300 and give their church my prayer list because He didn't want to hear from me any longer. I then proceeded to prophesy over everyone in the building. As I finished prophesying, Pastor Ricky took the microphone and spoke, "As You were praying for his people, the Lord told me to give you my Rolex watch."

I was so amazed: God had replaced my watch and given me a Rolex in four days! I called my wife and son on the way home, rejoicing and giving God praise all the way. Once I got home, I started really studying the watch and realized that it was not a blue-face Submariner. It was fake, fake, fake!

As I sat in amazement, I asked God why He would give me a fake Rolex. God abruptly told me that because of my attitude and my unwillingness to submit to His process, I was about to go birth a fake revival just like I got a fake Rolex. He then gave me instructions that I was not allowed to take this watch off my arm until it fell off. You cannot believe the humiliation of wearing a fake Rolex. I scraped it up and beat it against the concrete. I didn't want anyone to know that I had a fake Rolex.

That stinking thing turned green on my arm. Every day, God continuously spoke to me: "You want to do it my way and have a real move of my Spirit? Or do you want to have a fake revival that you'll have to sustain by yourself?"

He then said to me, "You've been asking for breakthrough anointing. But you have refused to let Me break you."

Kingdom Key: To have a breakthrough anointing, you must be broken first.

I started having encounters with the Holy Spirit that showed me what kind of ruler I was to become over the cities where I had been given responsibility. There was a prophet who was traveling around Hornell, New York, and the surrounding areas. I was receiving some unfavorable reports about his behavior. But the spiritual reports were that he was extremely prophetic and could hear the voice of God, and many said he reminded them of me and my ministry style.

I got a phone call from my nineteen-year-old niece. She started telling me about how a prophet called her out and gave her a prophecy that was almost word for word the same as one I had given her. Then she explained that this man who was over sixty years of age was not married, but had asked her to travel with him and do ministry. That was the final straw. I'd heard all the rumors, but those were all rumors. After I gave my niece very specific instructions not to travel with this man and to avoid him at all costs, I started to pray.

Three days later, in my morning prayers, the Lord asked this question: "How long are you going to tolerate this man's behavior in the city where I have given you responsibility?" He gave me clear instructions to confront him and tell him to leave. Responsibility will cost you!

Round 9: Who's in Charge: Father? Or Son?

I told the Lord, "This is not something you do over a cell phone." I was willing to get on an airplane and confront him. God spoke, "Since you're willing, be patient. I'll tell you what to do and what to say."

Two days later, I took a phone call from this man. He was in Orlando and wanted to come by my office. As we spoke, he told me he'd heard that I was a great prophet and had a great gifting. He wanted us to do a conference together.

With that invitation, I told him I would never share a pulpit with him.

I explained why, with some inside information from the Lord, and told him never to set foot in my city again. Five years later, the Lord asked me, "What kind of leader are you?" He asked me to try to bring reconciliation between him and several pastors in the city. I even set up the meeting, but he never showed up.

***

Kingdom Keys:

1. You can't have what you won't honor.
2. You can be a foundation to others and submit to their authority.
3. Don't judge the spirituality of others by your own gifting.
4. Don't let the sun go down on your wrath (and don't go to bed angry with your spouse).
5. The kingdom looks for ways to restore what was lost.
6. If you always use YOUR credit, God will never get HIS credit.
7. To have breakthrough anointing, you must be broken first.

Round 10

The Younger Brother!

You've already read the educational process God gave me through the business and my oldest son, Jason, yet I had no idea how God was going to use my younger son, Bryan. Of my two sons, Bryan is most like me. We both had a hard time with school, but both of us have overcome it. We both love people and loved being the life of the party.

Bryan, like his daddy, loves race cars and loves speed. He had a little four-cylinder, turbocharged Nissan that would absolutely fly. He would go to the racetrack or rebuild cars all over my garage. He had one for racing and another for daily driving. He had become a motor head, like I was in my teen years.

When he left to begin living on his own, he decided to move his girlfriend in with him, and they started playing house. Susie and I watched Bryan pull away from us as a family. We saw that things were definitely wrong in his life, and it was getting critical. This girl was absolutely demonic.

I can still hear Susie starting to fret: "Oh Lord, if she gets pregnant, we will have to put up with her. If she gets pregnant, she will ruin Bryan's life." The Lord prompted me to do the same thing with Bryan that I had done with Jason. I started praying Psalm 37:25. But this time, I prayed that he could keep his seed and it not be planted in the belly of the enemy's camp. I was waiting for the timing to be right. If I am like my Daddy God, I have to look for the right timing.

Church Fathers vs Kingdom Sons

When I choose the proper time, I will judge uprightly (Psalm 75:2).

Getting a Hold on Sin

Many years ago, the Holy Spirit dealt with me about Susie and the things she was doing that I considered "SIN." I was being very dogmatic about my convictions. He gave me a *rhema* word. I know it's taken out of context, but it has worked for me.

> Do not be rash with your mouth, and let not your heart utter anything hastily before God. For God is in heaven, and you on earth; therefore let your words be few (Ecclesiastes 5:2).

God told me that I am not the sin police and that what Susie was doing wasn't sin until He called it sin. He then told me to "shut up and love her." If the window of His longsuffering closed, He would let me know. Until then, the standard was love.

My whole family had begun to get really ticked off with me when I had pushed my weight around in the spirit realm. With the Holy Spirit's help, I had recovered a very broken marriage and a kid on crack, so why not now? Sometimes you get tired of being mocked and made fun of by your whole family. Was hell trying to have its way with me? It's harder to re-establish what it should have been when it never should have been broken in the first place. Look, if God had let me, I would have started over with some hot twenty-year-old who knew how to submit to me as ruler of my house. But King Jesus thinks He is in charge. It would have been easier, but not better.

I knew that I was in trouble with the Lord because I started to have an "I don't care" attitude about what was going on with my family. I was being l-a-z-y. Then, one morning, He asked me: "How long are you going to tolerate this in your household?"

Round 10: The Younger Brother!

Although Bryan was over twenty-one years old, according to kingdom principles he was still part of my household. "I'd never seen the righteous forsaken or my seed begging for bread" doesn't stop at twenty-one years old. So I told the Lord, "If this is the green light, and I need to deal with it, I'll do it. You open the door to his heart, and I'll 'git-r-done.'"

That afternoon, Bryan came by the store, and we went for a famous "walk with Dad." I asked him if I could see his driver's license. As I looked at it, I told him to look at his name: Bryan Charles Coker. I said, "Did you know that you're the son of a righteous man?"

He gave me one of those weird looks. "Yeah, Dad, I know I am."

"Bryan, do you love this girl that you're playing house with?"

"Yes, I do."

I asked, "Do you love her enough to marry her?" He replied that he didn't think so.

I told him that he was about to enter into a season where he was going to reap what he'd been sowing. If he did not marry this girl, there would not be a covenant between him and her; therefore, I could not go into the courts of heaven and get her born again. So I gave him very clear instructions: "You either marry her, or I'm going to start praying against her. Then you will have to bury her. She is demonic and is trying to destroy you and our family. I will not tolerate it any longer."

Bryan was all offended and angry with me. He called his older brother, the theologian, to tattle on me, and got his mother all riled up. That made me even more determined to drive that woman out of his life. She could go standing up or lying down in a box. She was going!

About five weeks later, Bryan came by the house and sat down on the couch. He wondered, "Dad, does heaven do what you ask it to do? Dad, three days after you told me what to do and I blew you off, we got into a fight. That crazy, demon-possessed girlfriend of mine flipped out and lost her mind. I knew at that point that I had to make a decision. I knew you were praying, and this wasn't working out very well for me. I want you to know she no longer lives with me."

Boy, was Susie happy to hear that! We could see Bryan was starting making better choices in his life, but he avoided me quite a bit. The youngest boy is always a mama's boy. (Like father, like son.)

Warning Dream

One night, a few months later, I had a prophetic dream. In this dream, a policeman knocking on my front door awakened me in the middle of the night. As I shook the officer's hand, I saw Bryan huddled in the corner by the door. I looked over the shoulder of the policeman and into the neighborhood. I saw many fires all around the neighborhood, except for my property, and I couldn't understand why my property had been spared.

The police officer said to me, "Mr. Coker, I recognize you're a man of great authority, but I have a problem with your son Bryan. He has been convicted of a crime, and he's going to be sentenced to prison." I questioned, "Are you positive that he is guilty?" He said, "Yes, look at all those fires. He is responsible for them all over the city, and it is a crime."

As I looked down at Bryan, he looked up into my eyes. I said, "Son, I've always tried to teach you if you're going to do the crime, you have to do the time."

The officer kept on: "Mr. Coker, you seemed a little distraught when I said that he had to go to the big house."

I spoke quietly. "Yes; in order to survive the big house, Bryan will have to harden his heart. If he hardens his heart in prison, he will not be able to hear God's voice, and therefore be unable to fulfill his dreams."

Round 10: The Younger Brother!

"Mr. Coker, I am a man of authority myself," he said. "I recognize that you also have tremendous authority, and I acknowledge from where you get your authority. Sir, I'll tell you what I can do. I have a friend who has a work camp. If I send Bryan to the work camp, he'll have supervision and oversight. He will be taught discipline so he will not have to harden his heart. He'll still be able to hear God's voice and fulfill his dreams."

I asked, "Would that fulfill the requirement of the judgment of his crime?"

"Yes."

"I mean, would he come out from the work camp with a clean slate and no record?"

He answered, "Yes, sir," and I said, "Sir, if you could do that, I would greatly appreciate it." He shook my hand.

When I woke up from this dream, my first question was, "What in the hell has this boy gotten himself into now?"

The following day, Bryan came by the office to get a check from his mommy because he had a dentist appointment. (I still don't know why we were paying his dentist bill.) I sat down and told Bryan about the dream that I had had.

As I was talking, Bryan said, "Dad, I know God speaks to you. I will take that as a warning." I said, "Bryan, I don't think you understand. It's not a warning. Judgment has already been executed. I am a righteous father, and I have tremendous authority. After this dream last night, I went to the courts of heaven and negotiated the boundaries of your judgment. It's up to you to make the corrections in your life." That "stern father" look came upon my face. I bellowed, "You had better straighten up and fly right. Do you hear me?!"

Several months later, Susie came to me. She felt like it was time for Bryan to move back home. I made the bold statement, "Absolutely not." We had peace in our home, and I enjoyed not having my children living with me. (I was going to build a one-bedroom house just so they couldn't come back.)

I could tell Susie wasn't happy with my answer, but I wasn't changing my mind. She waited a few weeks. One day she sat down with me and said, "Listen, I have something I want to talk to you about. I don't want you to give me an answer until you to pray about it."

I said, "What is it?"

She replied that she felt like it was time for Bryan to come back home. "He's making some choices and changes, and I believe he needs to get out of some situations. What do you think?"

I reminded her, "You told me to pray about it!"

A few nights later, we went to a house church meeting that was being held in our neighborhood. During worship, the Holy Spirit started speaking to me. "It is a privilege for a son to want to come back to his father's house. Bryan has made some good choices. He is now becoming teachable. Let him move back home and bless him."

I was sitting over in the corner, bawling like a big baby, tears running down my cheeks. Susie came and sat next to me. I told her what the Lord had said about Bryan.

Bryan coming home was a great thing. He definitely had become more teachable, and was pleasant to be around … except, he didn't clean his room when he lived there the first time, and some things never change.

Another Warning Dream

After several months, Bryan and Jason went to Jacksonville. THEY had decided that going in the army would be great for Bryan. I was completely out of the loop and had known nothing about it. Susie told me that he was enlisting and had gone to Jacksonville to be sworn in.

Round 10: The Younger Brother!

He got home about one thirty in the morning. We sat on the couch. I was curious: "Hey, I heard that you signed up for the army."

"Dad, I was going to." He was hesitant. "But I realized that I did not have your blessing, so I told the recruiter that I would be back." He asked for my blessing, and I gave it freely and lovingly. The army was the work camp where Bryan would find discipline and training and still be able to hear God's voice.

The following week, Susie and I went to Jacksonville with Bryan and spent the night there. Bryan got up at four in the morning, met his recruiter, and prepared to be sworn in. After he left the hotel room, I fell back asleep, and I had another prophetic dream about him.

In the dream, we were in a 747 airplane. As the plane was descending to land, I recognized that it was going to crash. Bryan was panicking, looking out the window. Everybody was terrified and screaming. Bryan looked at me and begged, "Dad, do something!" I unclipped my seat belt, stood up, pointed toward the cockpit, and yelled, "You'd better straighten up and fly right!"

After I told the plane to straighten up and fly right, the pilot gained enough control to land in an open field next to a baseball diamond. The plane skidded to a stop with the nose of the plane up against the backstop fence. A sign there read, "Field of Dreams."

The passengers started bailing out of all the emergency exits. We were all milling around in a state of awe because we were all safe. Suddenly, an FAA investigator was talking to the pilots and asking what had happened. The pilots reported that they knew the plane had been completely out of control. At the last moment, they gained enough response of the controls to do an emergency landing. They couldn't explain it! Bryan told the investigator, "I can tell you what happened. My father told this plane to 'straighten up and fly right.'"

The Lord had a word for Bryan before he left for Iraq. It was very difficult for me to give him. I let him know that when he came home,

Church Fathers vs Kingdom Sons

either he would have a tender heart and the ability to hear God's voice, or he would come home in a box. The choice was his.

I can remember the first phone call home from Iraq. "Dad, did you know that when the mortars are coming in over your head, that they actually whistle? I thought that was just something that happened in the movies. But they actually whistle."

"So what do you do when you hear them?"

He said, "I pull the covers over my head and pretend I'm in the fort and protected, like I used to at grandma's house."

Bryan had known Lori from school and church. They began to get serious when he came home on his first leave from Iraq. So when he called me from Iraq a year later and asked permission to marry her, I wasn't surprised. He was going to make sure they had my blessing, as he didn't want me to do what I had done to his last girlfriend!

They became officially engaged when Bryan came home, and we had a homecoming party at the home of Lori's mom and dad. My whole family was there. Friends and family of Lori's mom and dad were there. We had banners that said, "Welcome home!" on one side and "Congratulations!" on the other. Bryan had given his mother money to buy a diamond ring while he was in Iraq. (He should've known better: she spent $1,500 over his budget.)

As we were all toasting Bryan and Lori and their engagement, her father stunned us all (her parents weren't churchgoing people). He took the microphone and said, "The Lord works in mysterious ways." He started sharing that thirteen years earlier, he and his wife, Diane, were on the verge of a divorce. She had convinced him to go to a Valentine's Day banquet, where he heard a testimony about a man and woman whose marriage had been healed by God. He related that the impact of that testimony was so great that he and Diane were still married today.

That dinner was one of the first times Susie and I had publicly shared our testimony. We had no idea of its effects. Susie and I had had

Round 10: The Younger Brother!

a very bad fight over that speaking engagement because I had felt like God told me to speak, but I hadn't asked Susie before I confirmed. I had gotten bold with her, telling her I would stand in front of all those people and say that God had healed our marriage; I would also say her fear had gripped her so tight that she had threatened to walk out on our marriage again.

It took Susie thirteen years to understand that I had heard God, and she still didn't repent and tell me I was right. Because … God has a plan!

My son Bryan spent five years in the army. It was absolutely the best training of his life. Bryan came home from Iraq a man. He showed wisdom in the service and saved his combat pay. He bought a new car, purchased a house, and now has a precious baby girl (my cute granddaughter). He has finished his training to become a police officer and is now enrolled in college, finishing a degree in criminal justice. He is absolutely successful and never should be begging for bread.

> I have been young, and now am old; yet I have not seen the righteous forsaken, nor his seed begging bread (Psalm 37:25 KJV).

In Court with Jesus

A few days after the prophetic dream about Bryan and the airplane, I had another encounter with God. This was different from a prophetic dream: I was literally taken out of my body and seated in a courtroom setting. It wasn't a large public courtroom, but more of a council chamber. Those who were in the room had the responsibility of the city of Hornell, New York, as I do. Jesus was sitting at the head of the table with two others on each side. The Lord asked me a very simple question. He asked me, referring to the pastor in New York who had murdered my character and refused to forgive me for years, "Do you believe he has lost his ability to pastor the city?"

Church Fathers vs Kingdom Sons

I can remember deeply searching my heart to make sure that there was no criticism or judgment in me against this man so that when I answered the Lord, it would be pure and upright.

I confirmed to the council members in the room, "I believe this man totally loves Jesus. But his actions, lifestyle, and inability to bring correction to his marriage have left him without the influence to properly pastor this city any longer!"

I had just barely finished that statement when Jesus slammed down the gavel. He said, "It is decided: this man's mantle and responsibility are removed from this man to another." I knew to whom the mantle was shifting.

The process of this particular encounter caused me to ask the Lord what test I had passed that granted me access to sit in this place of authority in the courts of heaven. The Lord said, "Last week, when you properly judged your son, I knew I could trust you with a city."

In the kingdom of God, we function as Sons, Kings, and Priests. Sonship is our access; we judge as Kings; and we bring the proper sacrifices between heaven and earth to the mercy seat of God as Priests.

> And I bestow upon you a kingdom, just as My Father bestowed one upon Me, that you may eat and drink at My table in My kingdom, and sit on thrones judging the twelve tribes of Israel (Luke 22:29–30).

Handing the Baton

After this short season of not traveling to New York, I was in Hornell on vacation and ran into Brother Paul. He told me about a prophet who had called him out in North Carolina. This guy was very accurate about him personally and the church in Hornell.

During the conversation, he said that if he had the money he would have this guy come to the church and have some regional meetings.

Round 10: The Younger Brother!

I heard the Lord tell me to give him $1,500 to help support these meetings. Then the Lord had Susie and me fly up to be in the meetings. As I asked God what He was up to, He told me to be alert.

The night before we were to fly to New York I had a prophetic dream. In the dream, I was walking down a hallway in a suit coat with several people behind me. As I walked I saw a man, dressed about the same, coming to shake my hand. As our hands touched, we turned into track stars dressed in running clothes and running in a relay race in a large stadium. As I turned the corner, I handed him the baton. We successfully made the handoff.

He continued running, and the whole group—which had been running behind me—kept running after him. As I stopped on the track, I realized the group was made up of the friends, leaders, and people from the Hornell area to whom I had been ministering for years. I stood in the middle of the track trying to catch my breath while watching them run after this guy.

The Lord said, "What you have been running after is going to be handed to this prophet because the city wants a prophet and not Me. They can have what they want, but be on guard and protect them if you can."

When we arrived in Hornell, I finally met Gary, the man in the dream.

At the service that night, my wife was late coming into the meeting with my sister, Becky. I remember this part because I was a little ticked they were late.

This guy was off-the-chain accurate, and I was very impressive with his gift.

The next morning, we arranged a breakfast meeting with Gary, Susie, and me. We picked him up at his hotel. Susie sat in the back seat and asked Gary for a word. Susie has never been impressed with people who are prophets; she is married to one and has cleaned up behind me. She also has a very keen gift of discernment: "She don't have to know what's wrong to know something's wrong." She just does.

It was very unlike her to ask for a word.

Church Fathers vs Kingdom Sons

He started off, "Last night, when you came into the church late, I saw you in the spirit before you closed your heart to me. You're one hard-assed woman. You're not very impressed with the gifts."

He told her that he saw us arguing with me about her traveling in ministry when I needed her to come. That she was to be my protection from the traps of the enemy. He called out her gifting and then started to tell us that we were going to start a church. He told us we needed to have a church because it's the only way God would be able to train us.

He shared that he had made some very bad mistakes in his pastoring ministry a few years earlier. He gave me an example about a certain prophetic couple. The husband was a prophet, and his wife was a great prophetic worship leader from South Africa. They were some of the best he had ever been around. He told me that he had made some mistakes and hurt them and that I needed to have some life lessons like that also. He said that is why I need to pastor a church.

I asked later on if he had ever repented to this couple and if they were healed from the wounding that he had inflicted. His answer shocked me. He said, "Hell, I don't know. They left and went back to his hometown. That's not my problem anymore." So I asked where they lived, and he told me, "Deland, Florida." I asked their names, but the shocked look on my face was a small tip-off. After he found out I also lived in Deland, he never gave me their names.

So, for two years, God had me pray for the highly gifted couple who had been hurt by an ignorant prophet who was not man enough to ask their forgiveness and get them healed.

Well, as the dream showed, all of Hornell started running after this guy. He came back several times and preached in different churches. He put together a trip to Indiana that included some of the kids of the leadership of a church in town. God told me to make the trip and make sure that I was with the team at all times. Gary took his wife on this trip. She told me one day that she was glad I was in Gary's life and hoped he would take some of my advice.

Round 10: The Younger Brother!

I was sent by God to protect my Hornell kids from a predator prophet. Because I didn't explain myself to the leadership in Hornell, they automatically assumed I was best friends with this guy. He was starting to be exposed by God to Brother Paul and others.

Gary never wanted to build relationship after I called him on the carpet about the trip to Indiana.

After the two years of praying for this couple wounded by Gary, I was invited to a meeting in my home city of Deland, where I finally met Hank and his wife. The speaker at that meeting was Louis DeSiena, from Jacksonville. As he spoke, the Lord told me he was a kingdom apostle. I was in no frame of mind to hear that. But then the Lord told me that He was going to open the door for a relationship with Louis.

I had had it with self-proclaimed apostles, so I told God that if that were true, then he had to sow into my life first before I would consider a relationship with him. Louis called me out and gave me a word from the Lord. Then he went to his book table and gave me a copy of everything he had. At one time, I asked Louis to father me. Thank God for his wisdom to say no. We are brothers, and we are still in relationship today.

Hank and I have been friends for years now. He used my building for a season, then opened a church in Deland called Vivid Life Church. God has a plan to expand His kingdom.

***

Kingdom Keys:

1. When I choose the proper time, I will judge uprightly.
2. No judging until God closes the window of longsuffering.
3. A man's heart motives are more important than his gifting.
4. Taking responsibility includes protecting the innocent. It also includes good communication with those having the same responsibility.

Round 11

Sometimes the Fortune's Not What's inside the Cookie

A Trip to China with My Dad

The lighting company, under Jason's management, was growing at a tremendous pace. We opened a distribution center in Orlando. Our corporate office was in Orange City, and we started doing business with national builders. One day, I was making a delivery to one of them in Vero Beach. The Lord spoke to me at the intersection of Kings Highway and Route 60. He said to me, "I want you to open a lighting store in Vero Beach, because I want to restore your lost inheritance."

This didn't sit well with me because that was my hometown; our family goes back five generations in that county. Plus, it was the place of my shame: the adultery both Susie and I had committed that had threatened to tear apart our marriage had happened there for all the town to see. Truth be known, we had recovered from that season, but I did not want to deal with the demonic warfare that had taken me out before or face some of the people from the past. But the Lord said, "Restore My lost inheritance."

So I told Jason what God told me, and he started crunching numbers. He calculated how much gas, time, and energy we would use doing business over 100 miles away from our corporate office. He projected new growth, and he put a business plan together. So, we started looking for a location. We found a great location right on US Highway 1.

When God said He wanted to restore my lost inheritance, my carnal mind said, "I had a lot more money when I lived in Vero than I do now. Is God going to restore the finances I had lost? Spiritual thought … or is it for a greater purpose?"

We finished the construction of the showroom. The week we opened, I got a phone call from a Christian businessman I knew in Vero Beach. He started off by asking, "Charlie, how much does that billboard cost you a month?"

"What billboard?"

He said, "The billboard you just had put up beside your new showroom."

"Brian, I haven't paid for any billboard."

"It has to be yours."

I drove to the showroom for the first day of business in Vero Beach. I came in through the back door and unlocked the front door of the showroom. I looked to the right, and there was a huge billboard, painted all black, with a picture of Jesus. Below the picture was an inscription: "They will know them by their love one for another" (John 13:35). As I looked at this billboard, the Holy Spirit said to me, "Charlie, I've given you your billboard as a display to your hometown of the grace that is on your life." To my amazement, there was no name or phone number telling who had put this billboard up.

So I took a picture of it and sent it to Pastor Joe. Then I called him. I reminded him about the opportunity for billboards—what God had asked him to do and become a billboard of His grace—but I had gotten *my* billboard.

Round 11: Sometimes the Fortune's Not What's inside the Cookie

For over six months, that billboard was the talk of the town. Everybody thought I was the one who had put it up. For years it had been well-known that my marriage had been a public display of disgrace, but I had found Christ in a powerful way. Now, the whole town knew that I was back.

God has a funny sense of humor! I didn't know that I would start spending three nights a week at my dad's house. My father was having heart issues, and he had multiple surgeries. I have a sister in New York who is a registered nurse, yet God put me in the position of caring for him. This was all part of the plan of restoring my inheritance. A new relationship, at a spiritual level, with my father had begun to flower.

During this season, my father and I became very close. We started dealing with some of the hurts and wounds that had occurred over the years. After all these years, I still wanted my father's approval. I had finally gotten a blessing as his son, but he was unwilling to publicly declare that he was proud of me. "When you do business with the Son, you do business with me." The boxing match continued because we were in two different systems.

> For I have come to "set a man against his father, a daughter against her mother, and a daughter-in-law against her mother-in-law" (Matthew 10:35).

Church Fathers vs. Kingdom Sons!

One night, my father asked if I wanted to go to a special meeting that was taking place at New Hope Church, where he attends.

That night the guest speaker was Jack Taylor. He preached about the "Cosmos," with a PowerPoint presentation on how big God is. The Lord showed me that this man would become my spiritual father before God would release me into my true ministry calling.

Church Fathers vs Kingdom Sons

Whoopee! By this time I had been asking for over ten years, and I really didn't care. So I put God to the test by boldly stating, "If this is true, have Jack Taylor sow into my life first with no prompting from me."

After the meeting, when we were preparing to leave, Pastor Frank called me over to meet Jack and introduced me to him as a great young preacher. Papa Jack was very kind and friendly. He turned to his book table and gave me a book to read, but only if I promised to read it in the next thirty days. I promised, and we left.

While I was in bed that night, I asked God why I'd had to wait for a mentor or a spiritual father. He told me it's all about His timing. I complained that Jack had written several books, but he gave me someone else's book: *The Unshakable Kingdom and the Unchanging Person*, by E. Stanley Jones. (When Papa Jack got in my car eight years later and saw that I was reading that book, I had to admit that I never did read it within the promised thirty days. Confession is always good for the soul.)

My dad did admit that he had kept me at arm's length much longer than he should have. He wasn't sure about my positions and some of the challenges I exposed about the church system. He was a leader in the church system, and my gifting and overzealousness had become a threat to that. I think he was concerned about his reputation, but he asked me to forgive him for holding me at arm's length. I asked him to pray a father's blessing over me.

Needless to say, I had to pretty much walk him through it because he had never done that before. You see, when my grandfather died, my father was almost eleven. At the gravesite, he was told that he was now the man of the house and had to take care of his mother and brother. (What a load of garbage to dump on an eleven-year-old!) That made him a natural orphan, and he was responsible for himself and my emotional challenged uncle. My father dragged those orphan tendencies, which are always performance based to earn favor and blessing, into his spiritual walk.

Round 11: Sometimes the Fortune's Not What's inside the Cookie

In 2001 I asked the Lord to help me find the key to my father's heart. What he showed me was a man who beat my father when he was about thirteen years old. This man had married my grandmother and was a drunk. He stole two shotguns that my grandfather had left to my father. When I asked him who this man was, he opened a blue box he kept on the refrigerator and presented me with this man's obituary. He said some choice words about him in a way that showed me some of my father's wounds had not been healed. God was starting to knit our hearts together.

Now, my father is a man of tremendous integrity. He protected that upstanding character with a vengeance. He forced his children to flee all appearances of evil so that we would not disrespect the church or the things of God. But in my opinion, much of that was performance based and not heart driven. When the fear of man and man's opinion mold your behavior, it can become religious activity very quickly. One of the biggest resentments that I had against my father came because of a misunderstanding. When I was seven, the seventeen-year-old son of a deacon in the church sexually abused me at knifepoint. (He later died on death row for a double murder.) The deacon was a friend of my father's.

I told this man what his son had done to me, and he assured me that he would talk to my father and deal with the situation. For years, I thought my father had been told what had happened. But, he never communicated to my dad what actually happened. So I had the false assumption that my Dad had known and yet never protected me. I harbored great resentment because my whole life, I'd felt like I had taken one for the religious team so it wouldn't look bad for the church. I believe some of my anger toward the church stemmed from the bitterness that I held in my heart.

During the weekend in New York where I got in trouble at the church and called the pastor's wife a Jezebel and the pastor an Ahab, I shared my testimony in the men's group on Saturday morning. My father was there too, and after the meeting my dad said that he had never heard that story. But since I had carried that wound for over thirty years, I had a hard time believing that no one knew about the abuse I had suffered. My dad and I put a timeline together, and we figured it happened about the time the church was going through a church split and this deacon and my father were at odds, so nothing was ever said; meanwhile, the sense of abandonment I felt had simply festered, taking thirty years to heal.

All those years that I believed my father hadn't protected me, and that the abuse had been covered up to protect the church's reputation, finally make sense.

My father is a man's man, and he was a strong father in the culture and environment of our home. As a result of the abuse when I was seven, a homosexual spirit tried to entrap me during my teenage years. Because I had a strong father in the home, I leaned to heterosexual pornography and not homosexuality. (I will explain in more detail in *From Rape to Righteousness: Redeeming the Bride of Christ*.) I believe the reality of Sonship and the father's blessing can and will heal sexual brokenness and homosexuality. I have personally witnessed the power of a spiritual father praying a blessing over a son, which brought deliverance from the tormenting homosexual spirit that the son had been battling.

> **The reality of Sonship and the father's blessing can and will heal sexual brokenness and homosexuality.**

Speaking the Word in China

I wondered how all of this was restoring my inheritance. But when a father and son can deal with the root issues, get healed, and bless one another, the inheritance of the kingdom manifests in a powerful way.

It was about this time that the Lord spoke to me and said, "You are in training and are learning to father your father." I can remember

Round 11: Sometimes the Fortune's Not What's inside the Cookie

spending hours talking to Dad about wanting to be in full-time ministry. He repeatedly reminded me that being in business was ministry. I was fruitful, impacting people's lives and expanding the kingdom. Due to his church mindset, he couldn't see how I fit or how I would ever be successful in a church setting. Let's face it: at this point, I didn't have a pastoral bone in my body. Based on my history, I hadn't been accepted or successful in that system, but I knew the calling was like fire shut up in my bones.

By now, it had been ten years since my mother had passed away. Betty, my dad's girlfriend, has a son who is a missionary to China. My dad started putting a trip together with Mama Betty and his pastor, Frank. The Lord asked me if I would go to China and look after my father. His health was actually in pretty good shape at the time, so I had a feeling God was up to something.

As we boarded the airplane for our eighteen-hour flight to Hong Kong, the Holy Spirit asked me to take some time and read all of the Minor Prophets; I took out my Bible and I started reading. At the conclusion of reading all the Minor Prophets, the Lord asked me what I saw. I said Lord, "What I see in Scripture is a divided kingdom. What I see is a northern tribe and a southern tribe. Lord, what I see is two triangles. Just like America, Israel was divided."

This trip to China was exceptionally beautiful. Betty's son, Pete, had lived there for twenty years, so he was the best tour guide money could buy. Traveling with Pastor Frank and his wife, my father and his girlfriend Betty, and a few other people, we were having a great time.

Pete took us to work with some of the underground churches. We saw what he had been doing through the educational system, building relationships, and expanding the kingdom. It was exciting to see what God was doing in this land. He then took us to an aboveground church that was several hundred people strong. Showing your passport was required to visit in this church, so the congregation mostly consisted of missionaries and other foreigners.

Church Fathers vs Kingdom Sons

The morning before we went to this church service, the Lord had given me a vision about a ripped net. Fish were escaping the holes in the net. As the Lord showed me this vision, I knew the net had not been repaired, although it could have been. Because of relationships that were broken due to offenses and an unwillingness to ask for forgiveness, the great harvest was slipping away.

On the way to the church meeting, the Holy Spirit told me that He wanted me to release a word. He said, "Tell them to fix the broken relationships, or I will send some of them home. Remind them that this is not the first time I have brought this situation to the leadership."

I started pleading with God, "Please don't make me do this in front of my father." I told God how much he despised it when a prophet gives a word of correction, especially me.

The Lord God was stern when He asked me if I feared Him more than my father. The Lord knew the answer to that, but I was trying to weasel out of it. I made a deal with God that I would not tell anyone that I had this word, and that He had to supernaturally put the microphone in my hand.

As the preacher was preaching his message at the church meeting, he stopped in midsentence, pointed at me, and asked, "Prophet, do you have a word?"

I took the microphone and explained the vision that I'd had that morning, telling them that the revelation was that they had broken relationships within the body there and with other churches in the city. I told them that the Lord was bringing this out publicly because they had refused to deal with it when it was brought to them privately.

After church, we all went to lunch. When we returned to our hotel room, as the door closed behind me, my father decided it was time to reprimand me. He asked me, "Who in the heck do you think you are?" He then challenged the word that I gave. I acted like an eight-year-old and shut down. But in my heart, I made a decision. I told God I was

Round 11: Sometimes the Fortune's Not What's inside the Cookie

never going to allow myself to be in a position where my father could dominate and control what I did when it came to the matters of the kingdom. I looked at my Dad with tears in my eyes and said, "I think you were happier with me when I was running around in the bars. You prayed for me to get saved, but I think I got saved more than you like."

That was the day I made the decision to stand against the religious, controlling spirit that my father had used to manipulate me my whole life.

Several days later, Pete took us to work with some underground churches. One of the leaders from the church where I had released that word was there, and he asked if he could speak with me privately; I told him it was okay to say whatever he wanted to in front of my father. He let me know that the word that I had released was very accurate, and it was not the first time they had heard it. But the leadership said that they would replay the word and fix each broken relationship as God revealed it. Then he thanked me for my boldness.

My dad looked at me and said, "Well, I feel silly." As I looked at my father I said to him, "And the problem is, you think that's the first time."

On this particular trip I was having a hard time containing my zeal, and that kind of irritated my father. He felt like I was dominating every conversation with some new fresh revelation, but that's what we do as orphans:

Kingdom Key: "It is not good to have zeal without knowledge, nor to be hasty and miss the way" (Proverbs 19:2 NIV).

I didn't know God was about to deal with the issue of unsanctified zeal within my life. But the revelation of zeal without knowledge was one of the major steps in my healing.

Church Fathers vs Kingdom Sons

We had a great time in China and boarded the plane to head back home. As I sat in my seat, rehearsing the events of the trip with the Lord, He asked me how I saw the condition of the church in China. I'd always heard that the underground house churches of China had become the new role model of what God was doing on the earth. What I saw in the house churches there definitely has a place and can be effective in expanding the kingdom. There is also a huge aboveground church in China, but the two are divided.

I saw two completely separate triangles, with the house church as one triangle and the aboveground church as the other: two triangles never to find the holy sweet spot in the middle where they blended. As I pondered this, the Lord spoke to me. "I want to show you what I'm about to do on the earth."

I went into a vision. I saw the two triangles under extreme pressure get mashed together, and as the two triangles came together I saw that they formed the Star of David. And then in the middle of the Star of David I saw a picture of Christ in the middle. The Lord said, "Charles, the body of Christ is leaving the church age, and I'm in the process of birthing the kingdom. The old system still has foundational principles from which I can bring my kingdom." He then said that the older would serve the younger.

He said the church had entered into the same season as when John the Baptist started crying in the wilderness. He asked me, "Why haven't you asked Me why I had John the Baptist's head cut off?" I asked the Lord if He actually did that. I thought Satan did it. He then informed me that He was sovereign.

The Lord told me that John the Baptist was the end of the Old Testament prophets and Jesus was a transitional prophet from the old to

Round 11: Sometimes the Fortune's Not What's inside the Cookie

the new. He had John the Baptist's head cut off so that when he gave the baton to Jesus, it would be headless—Christ is the head of the church.

He also told me to warn the arrogant and prideful pastors that He's going to start coming with a sword, just like He did in the days of John the Baptist, and for them to be careful and not lose their heads.

The Lord then asked me if I would go home and start a church. He said that He would give me discernment about the people I needed as a pastor and show me different areas in their lives where I could bring healing and insight to their destinies, which is the triangle with the point up. God would also give me discernment about the strengths where I needed to get underneath and apostolically push them up, with the triangle point down. He gave me the name of the church: "One Kingdom Fellowship."

I told the Lord that I did not have the strengths and capabilities to do it, and I did not have the grace to be a pastor. The Lord told me that He would give me the grace to pastor, but I would be functioning as an apostle in the ministry. He'd given me Pastor Rodger to co-pastor with, and that he would function as a prophet. We would become an apostolic and prophetic team.

We landed at Orlando International Airport. We stood at the curb, hugging and kissing, getting ready to go our separate ways. I hugged my father and whispered in his ear, "Dad, if you ever again usurp the spiritual authority God has given me, the next time He asks me if it's time for you to go home to be with Him in heaven, I will tell Him, 'Yes, take him.' I love you and I respect you, but don't undermine my authority again when I'm operating in my gifting." That day the control was broken. And the authority shift happened.

He Took Away the Zeal

A couple of weeks after we had gotten home from the China trip, I was at my Dad's house I couldn't sleep, so rather than toss and turn, I got up at 1:30 a.m. and drove home. Halfway home, in the pitch dark on I-95, I started weeping and crying. I asked the Lord what sin I had committed that made me lose my zeal for Him. The Lord asked me why I thought I had sinned.

"Holy Spirit, it must be a sin that would make me lose my zeal for you."

Then the Lord spoke to me and said, "No, son, *I* took your zeal for Me away!"

I then asked, "Why in the world would You take that away?"

"I have been trying to take you to a place of maturity," He answered. "I had to remove your zeal *for Me* to make room to deposit the zeal *of Me*."

This was the beginning of my path to Sonship. Sonship learns to lean back and work *from* inheritance instead of working *for* your inheritance. When you're an orphan, you use your energy and zeal for Him in the hopes that you're pleasing Him. Sonship has the zeal of Him and true relationship as a Son; therefore, you do the Father's business with His blessing. This does not require nearly the energy.

> **When you're an orphan, you use your energy and zeal for Him in the hopes that you're pleasing Him. Sonship has the zeal of Him and true relationship as a Son; therefore, you do the Father's business with His blessing.**

It was about this time that the Lord gave me a vision of a triangle that covered Florida. It started north of Jacksonville, proceeded down the east coast to about Stuart, went west over to the Tampa area, and back up to northern Florida. Right in the middle of the triangle is where I live in central Florida. I started a campaign just like I had done in New York, and I have driven to every town and every village. As I traveled, I

Round 11: Sometimes the Fortune's Not What's inside the Cookie

repented for the sins of the church and of the leadership, and asked God for revival. It was obvious He was giving me responsibility in the area of the triangle and wherever He would send me; I would have authority in the kingdom realm.

Please don't think that I'm all that and a bag of chips. I know that I'm only one of perhaps hundreds of people God has called within this triangle to do their part. But where the King is giving us responsibility, the kingdom is starting to expand within those borders of authority.

***

Kingdom Keys:

1. "It is not good to have zeal without knowledge, nor to be hasty and miss the way" (Proverbs 19:2 NIV).
2. You transform from zeal *for* God to the zeal *of* God.

Round 12

Birthing the Church

For many years, Pastor Rodger and I had talked about starting a church together. He'd been my pastor at Trinity. Then he became the associate pastor under Pastor Joe. After he'd been in that position a few years, the Lord gave me a revelation that the ministry was taking a toll on Rodger's marriage and asked me to give Rodger a job at my lighting store. I told the Lord I didn't have a position for him at that time, but was willing to do whatever He told me to do.

Rodger and I went to a prophetic training school at Bishop Bill Hamon's in northern Florida. While we were riding back, I shared the revelation with him that God had given me. The Lord had told me that if I didn't get him out of the ministry, his marriage was in trouble. So, we made the decision that he would come to work for me. The week we were gone, my warehouse manager turned into Mr. Stupid and cussed out one of my best customers; he was fired, so Rodger took his place the following week.

Kingdom Key: When the foundation of love supports the archway of honor, then the door of God's favor opens to you!

Pastor Rodger had become my best friend and spiritual confidant. He was also my pastor, to whom I submitted. Now I was his boss, and he had to submit to me. Then we added my oldest son, Jason, into the mix, and we both had to submit to him at work. Jason submits to us at church.

When there are multiple arenas of authority, you have to be careful not to cross those lines. And when you do, you need to address them and fix them. Most people want authority, but few take responsibility for that authority.

> **Kingdom Key: You only have authority in the areas where you have taken responsibility.**

You can find people's authority by looking at what responsibility they've taken upon themselves. Too many church people want a title to give them authority but have never taken the responsibility in the realm of the spirit or the natural. Pastor Rodger and I experienced this years ago when we were doing the house church and deliverance ministry. I continued to submit to him, because he had been my spiritual authority, instead of taking my rightful place and leading. One time when a crisis manifested, checks had to be written, responsibility taken, and hard decisions made, Rodger checked out and vanished for three days, leaving me to make the hard decisions. I made them because I was responsible for the outcome, resulting in an authority shift in our relationship.

> **Kingdom Key: During an authority shift, there is at least a three-day death and resurrection process. If you allow this three-day disconnect to be Holy Spirit led, you can reconnect, properly aligned.**

If the body of Christ would actually learn this principle, people would not split churches to become promoted in the kingdom.

Arguing with God

I went on a forty-day water-only fast. During this time, the Lord started debating with me about starting the church. We argued for thirty-

Round 12: Birthing the Church

nine days. You can only argue with God so long before He pulls His God card and tells you, "You will obey me." (For some reason, He thinks He's God!) I explained to the Lord that my company was attached to the building trade in Florida, and it was heading into the economic toilet very quickly. There was absolutely no way I could financially support a church!

I know every good pastor starts in faith and obedience, but I'm not one of them. I was a strong-willed, opinionated orphan who loved God with all my heart, but I was fighting Him every step of the way. So I decided to negotiate with God and see if He was serious about this church stuff. I told Him that because the church had been financially raped, I was not going to stand in a pulpit every Sunday and beg for tithes and offerings. I told Him if He was serious, He had to give me the money up front so that all the bills would be paid for at least two years. None of this "blind faith" stuff. If He did that, I would know He was serious.

I finished the forty-day fast, then I sat down with Jason and Susie and told them what the Lord had said. Immediately both of them responded with record-breaking negativity: "Dad, we're struggling in the business." "Charlie, you don't have one pastoral bone in your body. You don't even like churches." While all that was true, I told them that I had made a deal with God. If He would pay for it up front, then I would do it. "What are the chances of God doing that?" I thought God would bail on the whole thing.

There was a businessman who owned a shopping center in Deltona. In the corner of that shopping center, George and Judy Jones had had a church for over five years. At one time, I had actually gone to that church and been part of their fellowship. Judy had run a community outreach center there for nine years. The businessman decided to sell the shopping center, but the purchaser wanted the space to have a three-year tenant in the corner. Judy had been offered another building by the city. I learned all this information later. The businessman told me he felt that I was to have a church in that building and gave me over $225,000 to pay the rent.

Yeah, that was a "Jehovah Sneaky."

To my surprise, God was actually serious about me starting a church. My heart and passion were to travel; I had been functioning in the triangle of authority in New York on and off for sixteen years, and he had shown me a triangle of authority in Florida. But, pastoring? Lord, You've got be kidding!

The Lord was bringing revelation about starting the church. He had shown me that the government structure always comes in threes—Father, Son, and Holy Spirit; Abraham, Isaac, and Jacob; and finally apostle, prophet, and teacher.

> **Kingdom Key: Anytime you find government, you will find three elements within the principle.**

So, God was trying to design and facilitate this church thing. I started asking the Lord how it was going to work with Rodger and me. Rodger is the most loving, kindest pastor you've ever met in your life. I'm a raw prophet trying to go through the death process of becoming an apostle. God's been trying to teach me this. Because of my orphan thinking and insecurities, I believed that if I didn't have Rodger with me, I would be weak and ineffective as a leader: just like I felt I needed a partner at the store. Rodger was pastoral, and I knew I needed that.

I went into a vision. The Lord revealed that when Rodger was young, he had had a prophetic word given to him that went something like this: "You will function as a pastor, but in your latter years you will operate as a prophet." I brought this revelation to Rodger. He totally confirmed that it was from God because he had not shared that with anyone. In

Round 12: Birthing the Church

this model, I'm to function as an apostle, Rodger was to function as a prophet, with my son Jason serving as the teacher. This structure works:

> And in the church God has appointed first of all apostles, second prophets, third teachers, then workers of miracles, also those having gifts of healing, those able to help others, those with gifts of administration, and those speaking in different kinds of tongues (1 Corinthians 12:28 KJV).

A New Season

During the time God was preparing me to start a church, I had credentials with an apostolic network. So I called my overseer, looking for some counsel on how to pioneer a church. After about eight or nine phone calls, I realized I was either being ignored or God was shutting the door. Since I believe in authority, I believe in submitting to authority, and I wasn't getting a clear answer, I prayed and asked the Lord what was going on.

He asked me what the official start date for the lease was. I told Him January 1, 2008. He inquired, "When do your credentials need to be renewed?" I pulled out my credentials card and saw that the renewal date was January 1, 2008. The Lord then said to me, "This is a new season of your life, and I'm going to bring men into your life who will be counsel to you, father you, and teach you the things that you do not know."

I no longer had a spiritual authority to submit to—a totally new concept for me—and in some ways, that was quite scary. If you are burdened by true insecurities and still think like an orphan, there are many pitfalls that can be avoided by listening to those who have been down the same road. The Lord told me that the blueprint for me to build on was already inside of me, and I would need to walk it out day by day.

Rodger and I decided that the genuine structure would be the apostle/prophet positioning between us, but publicly we would co-pastor as equals. I had no problem with that because I was totally secure in his ability to hear God and to make decisions. We had learned to trust one another over the previous eighteen years both as co-workers and friends. Many doubters believed that there couldn't be two heads and this would never work. People would then ask how things worked between our wives and us. Privately, Rodger and I never made a decision that we did not agree on. That was a great safety net for me, as it helped cover my insecurities and fears.

Rodger had a tremendous seer gift. He saw angels and all kinds of things in the spirit realm. He was great at the prophetic, and all those years in which he served as a pastor made us a great team. He had been on dozens of missionary trips to Russia and all over Europe. He'd been to South America and the Dominican Republic numerous times. Rodger even took a year off, while he worked at the store, to become a missionary trainer in the Bahamas with a friend of ours. He would light up like a Christmas tree on the mission field. He took some of our leaders on a mission trip to Honduras. They saw thousands of people saved, blind eyes opened, deaf ears healed, and even a dead baby come back to life.

We adopted the logo of the two triangles coming together in forming One Kingdom, and that's how we structured our leadership. The first few years were an absolute joy. During that time, I traveled to New York and Pennsylvania. While I was gone, Rodger was at the church preaching and pastoring, the perfect fit.

Breaking Bad Vows

Pastoring week to week was much more difficult than I ever imagined. Trying to pastor people who were hurt and wounded was starting to take a toll on me. So, one day in prayer, I asked the Lord to help me to become a better pastor. His answer shocked me. The Lord let me know that He couldn't help in that department because of my own words. I then went to a vision and overheard myself speaking, "I'm not a pastor, I will never pastor, and I don't even like most pastors." The Lord said to me, "You made a vow that I cannot break. Until you

Round 12: Birthing the Church

break the vow, I cannot release the pastoral grace and anointing that you need to minister to my people." So I started asking for forgiveness and breaking the vow.

Kingdom Key: Don't make stupid vows you have to renounce later.

It was amazing! I even started liking the children. The Lord reminded me of an incident when I was in Pastor Carlos's church. I was walking through the kitchen, and there were two young boys who were absolute hoodlums in our church. Pastor Carlos was on the floor wrestling with both of them, and as I walked by one boy said, "Pastor, Pastor: See that man right there? He doesn't play." Even though that was true, it broke me to repentance.

Our church attracted several strong women who were very gifted and others who were much wounded. When I look back at this, I see that it was God sending people that the church system had rejected. These were women with control issues, hurt by husbands or religion, but God was changing my heart and had given me the insight to their destinies.

I became very patient compared to how I used to be. To my own detriment, I started to tolerate things that I shouldn't have, but I could see their God-given callings. God was starting to break my heart and give me a love that I previously did not have. Many years ago, God gave me a vision of a large army of women ushering in the great harvest of souls. This helped me understand why I was molding all these gifted women.

I would have to say that at least 75 percent of the time, Rodger and I would come to church, compare notes, then "tag preach." By honoring each other's gifts and talents, we were demonstrating the kingdom at a level that many had never seen. We are all interdependent on each other. This is shown as we appreciate each other's uniqueness and learn to depend on each other.

An Unusual Worship Team

When Rodger and I started the church we knew the key would be worship, so we started praying for a worship leader sent by God. At one point, we got desperate enough that we tried to hire a guy from Alabama. That didn't work. So, in my frustration, I started praying one day about it.

The Lord broke into my prayers and said, "The problem is that you want your version of a worship team, not the one that I want."

So I asked Him, "What do You want for a worship team?"

I went into a vision where there were nine warehouses. The ninth warehouse garage door was open, and inside was a heavy metal band. They were playing the most god-awful, growling, loud music I'd ever heard. I despised it. As I was walking up to the band, the guys asked, "Can we help you?" I said, "Yes, I am Pastor Charlie Coker from One Kingdom Fellowship. I want you guys to come on Sunday and lead worship at my church." They all started laughing and said they were not Christians. "I will take care of that in a minute, but on Sunday I want you to come and do worship." They were smoking and drinking, and had tattoos all over their bodies. I led them to the Lord; in the vision, they became my worship team.

I couldn't believe this was God's choice! It totally exposed my religious judgments and criticisms. I released this word for six or eight weeks to the church. Then one Sunday morning, I looked at the second row. The Lord reminded me what they looked like. I started picking them out: "You're the lead singer with flames on your guitar, you're the bass player, and you're the drummer." I led them all to the Lord that day.

The next Monday night, they came to practice and were completely surprised that they could play normal music. Pastor Rodger was actually there with them, and they were shocked at the anointing that showed up in the room. The name of their band was Hog Breeders. They changed

Round 12: Birthing the Church

the name to Thorns of the Crown. They practiced on Thursday night, and by Sunday morning they were our worship team.

Some of my leaders and I went to a place called the Dungeon. We were amazed how those in the heavy metal culture honored each other and waited for each other to play and interact. I saw more kingdom in that culture than I had seen in the church. The success of Thorns of the Crown led the manager of the Dungeon to start having Christian heavy metal bands night once a quarter.

We had Christian heavy metal bands come to the church for concerts. My father came to the church when we were having one. I figured he would absolutely lose it, but he didn't. He only made one small suggestion. He said, "Son, if I were you, I would put the words of the songs on the overhead so that people could read the words and know they're talking about God. Otherwise, they will think it is demonic."

Offenses Taken

Our children's department began to grow, and soon we were in need of a children's pastor. About this time, Rodger's wife came into the church on a Sunday morning and said she had a warning dream with me in it. She said that in the dream, I had made Rodger the children's pastor, taken the lead role, and demoted Rodger to be my associate. She told me that that was never going to happen! We were co-pastors; they had done children's ministry long enough and were never going to do it again.

Pastor Rodger and his wife became offended with some of the decisions I was making, and I don't think we ever recovered from that first offense. The problem was, Rodger was my best friend. I loved him dearly, and I truly did not know what to do. Any decisions I made were going to hurt our relationship, and because of my insecurities, I believed I would not be successful without him.

The boxing match between church fathers and kingdom sons was starting to happen between us. I knew it was happening between my father and me, and I had experienced it between Jason and me. But I didn't realize till later that it was happening between Rodger and me. I was starting to grow up and take my rightful position privately, which I've always done. But now it was public, and that is where the fight always begins.

I know this is not a Bible verse, but you've heard the phrase, "All good things must come to an end."

Decision Time

I started taking trips, focusing my efforts and attention on New York and Pennsylvania, and that started to take its toll on One Kingdom. (The vision that God gave me in 1996 about a move of God showed revival where the glory cloud of God shows up and people are instantly converted to the King of Kings and Lord of Lords.) I still can't get this promise from God out of my head. I don't want to go back any longer and start my own man-made revival. I want the real deal. Lord knows I don't want another fake Rolex.

The Lord had been speaking to me about going back to New York when an invitation came with a specific date. As I pondered this request to go preach, I asked the Lord if this was still practice or if this was the real season and the right timing for the release of the kingdom. He assured me this was no longer practice. I had entered into the season of no return. Being bold, I said to Him, "You promised me a Harley and a Rolex on that mountaintop in 1996 as a sign of the coming season of revival. When you give me the Harley, then I'll go back to New York and preach!"

Several days later, my wife asked if I had bought my airplane tickets for New York, and I informed her that I had decided I would not go to New York until I got my Harley-Davidson motorcycle. She started, "I know what you're going to do. You'll wait until the last minute. God will speak to you, and then you will pay three times what you should for your airplane ticket." I said, "No, if I don't get my Harley I'm not going. I preach every Sunday. I don't need a place to preach anymore,

Round 12: Birthing the Church

and I don't need any more practice. If God is not going to do His part, I'm no longer doing mine."

About three days later, a friend of mine named Randy who owned a beautiful Harley called me up and said, "Charlie, I'm going to China to be a missionary and will be gone at least two years." The worst thing you can do to a Harley is let it sit and not use it … He brought me his Harley and the title, and said we'd figure out what to do when he got back. Well, armed with my new Harley, I bought my airplane ticket. I started returning to New York on a more regular basis.

It was time to start making some decisions about the business. The economy was not doing well, my oldest son's marriage was coming apart, and my daughter-in-law was planning to move to Miami with my grandson. From July to December, I traveled through New York and Pennsylvania, doing more ministry there than I did at home. Susie and I decided to go to New York for our Christmas vacation.

Christmas Eve day, before we got on the airplane, a Christian businessman friend called me and wanted to have a cup of coffee. During our conversation he said that he had an encounter with the Lord about me. The Lord had shown him who I was and that I carried a Sons of Issachar anointing, since I understood the times and the seasons like they had. He also said that the Lord told him to give me a special Christmas present that I was not to open until Christmas day.

Before we went on vacation, I had told Susie that we had to make some major decisions about staying in business. My son Jason was definitely going to move to Miami, the economy was in shambles, and this burning desire for full-time ministry was consuming me. The Lord had told me that He would take care of us. He could give me an employee to replace Jason, or we could close the business with bankruptcy, trust God, and do ministry full-time. I told Susie that she needed to make the decision. Whatever I did, I was not going to bring her kicking and screaming into full-time ministry.

Church Fathers vs Kingdom Sons

We decided to open the Christmas present instead of putting it in our luggage. To our surprise, when we opened up a little box, there sat my blue-faced Submariner Rolex. I now had the Harley and the Rolex. God was saying, "This is the season to trust Me."

Closing the business has been one of the hardest things I've ever had to do. I made things happen because of the business. I wrote my own checks, and I set my own schedule. I believe in some ways it had become my identity. God was about to change all of those things.

***

Kingdom Keys:

1. When the foundation of love supports the archway of honor, then the door of God's favor opens to you!
2. During an authority shift, there is a three-day death and resurrection process. If you allow this three-day disconnect to be Holy Spirit led, you will reconnect being properly aligned.
3. Any time you find government, you will find three elements within the principle.
4. Don't make stupid vows you have to renounce later.
5. Kingdom name of God: "Jehovah Sneaky"
6. You only have authority in the areas where you have taken responsibility.

Round 13

You Don't Know Jack, Until You Know Jack

After getting the Harley and the Rolex, which were signs from God that Susie and I were in the season where He's moving, I spent more time in New York ministering in the triangle of authority from Buffalo to Syracuse and down to Hornell.

I felt like the apostle Paul on my third missionary trip. The first time, I functioned within the church system. The second time, I was in an apostolic prophetic house church movement. And this time, I believed I was coming with a fresh blueprint of kingdom principles.

Moses received his pattern (blueprint) after being on the mountain of God.

> And see to it that you make them according to the pattern, which was shown you on the mountain (Exodus 25:40).

For each of us to have the right blueprint, we must get it from the same mountain of God that Moses did. What I came to realize was that I'd been missing some of the main elements of the blueprint that I was carrying.

To the Third and Fourth Generation

I decided to take an extended road trip and go to a conference in Erie, Pennsylvania, where Leif Hetland was speaking. After one of my friends in New York told me about this conference, the Lord spoke to me and told me to go. I had scheduled a meeting with a bishop from Buffalo that was in town, so my leaving town was pushed back to later Thursday morning. I decided to go to the meeting and then just drive all night to get to Pennsylvania for the conference.

At this breakfast meeting, I shared with him my insight on the next move of God, which I believed would come out of Buffalo. I explained that when I was in Africa with Dr. Richardson, I had a vision that America was about to have a move of God's Spirit, not because of repentance, but because of time.

Studying the Charles Finney revival that started in Rochester, New York, shows it spread from Buffalo east to Syracuse and then south to Hornell. That particular revival should have spread to the whole nation, but it stopped fifty miles south of Rochester and had very little effect from there. While I was in Africa, God showed me a vision of the leadership of that revival, which hadn't dealt with racial issues and divisions in the church. Their sin stopped this move of God from going national. The Lord told me the sins of the father affect the third and the fourth generation, and that the fruit of that leadership group was gone. Since the influences of the previous generations had died, America was about to see a fresh move of the Spirit.

I asked the Lord, "Why Buffalo, one of the cities instrumental to the end of slavery over 160 years ago?" He showed me that Buffalo was the final gateway of the Underground Railroad for African slaves to escape America and find freedom. God said, "The gateway that the African slaves used to find freedom will be the gateway He uses to bring true freedom back to America."

After this encounter alongside a cannon in the courtyard of the Elmina slave castle in Ghana, I came home and preached that America should prepare for black leadership. I thought it would be in the church, and I was very involved with the Promise Keepers movement to bring reconciliation to the church and the country. But when Barack Obama became my president, I was puzzled because I had misread that this

Round 13: You Don't Know Jack, Until You Know Jack

was a national word and not limited to the church. The first foreign trip he took was to the slave castles in Ghana. I have a picture of Anderson Cooper doing an interview with him, standing next to the same cannon in the courtyard of the Elmina slave castle.

This trip to Ghana was life-changing for me. God showed me the spiritual roots of racism. I was given a statement from the Lord about black leadership coming into power: "Because of the cross of Jesus Christ, there is no greater sin than to commit the sin that was committed against you." And for over eighteen years I have been pushing to empower black leadership within the churches in the cities that I had influence.

As I explained this to Bishop, he got a little excited since he owned the property, which was the end of the Underground Railroad in Buffalo's inner city.

This is a little premature in this timeline, but let me add this: Toward the end of Barack Obama's first term, I had a vision where the Lord took me to stand in front of the statue of Abraham Lincoln in Washington. While I looked at the statue, the Holy Spirit said, "The assignment I gave Abraham Lincoln for this nation is about to come to an end. And then I'm going to turn this nation upside down with my glory."

The Lord showed me that the division of our nation is a mirror image of the division of His church. I believe God holds the leadership of His church responsible for the condition of this nation. The spirit of entitlement, which has become entrenched in the core belief systems of America, came into power because the church has been unwilling to deal with the entitlement mentality within its own walls. (This is a nationwide orphan spirit released by the church.)

Finding the Spiritual Father

Needless to say, after meeting with the bishop I was definitely itching to get on the road. I love being on the road; I seem to have some

Church Fathers vs Kingdom Sons

of my greatest encounters with the Lord on these trips. I was scheduled to be gone twenty-one days.

While I was driving in the dark mountains of West Virginia, about midnight one night, Jesus manifested and sat in the seat behind me. He started talking to me about some things going on in my life. When I asked Him why He didn't sit in the front seat, He laughed. "Where would I sit?"

(That's an inside private joke between us. You see, years ago, I was praying and asked Jesus to manifest, sit down in my car seat, and talk to me like a man. He told me that I didn't have room for Him because I had three Bibles and six teaching tapes all about Him. I had made no room for Him to sit and talk because I was too busy trying to learn *about* Him instead of learning *from* Him.)

I said, "Lord, I can make room very quickly."

"No, I'll sit right here so I can talk into your ear."

As we were talking about the season from which I was emerging, He asked me if I liked the Rolex watch He had given me. "Of course I like this watch. It's a blue-faced Submariner, worth about $10,000. It's what I had always wanted. I could've bought one for myself, but You had made a promise to give it to me as a sign. Plus, it's from You."

He said, "I'm glad you like it. (My first thought was, "Oh dang it, He's going to ask me to give it away.") But when you go to this conference tomorrow, you will find a man with an identical watch on his wrist. When you find him, give him your business card and tell him to have Jack Taylor call you. It's time to get into relationship with the man that I promised you seven years ago. I promised he would father you before you entered into the ministry that I have called you to."

I arrived in Erie only a few hours before the meetings began. The conference speaker for the first night was Leif Hetland. As he went to minister, he stretched his arms and told a story about how he had just spent two weeks in Florida with his spiritual father, Jack Taylor. Imagine

Round 13: You Don't Know Jack, Until You Know Jack

my reaction when a blue-faced Submariner Rolex popped out from his sleeve! Sometimes you wonder if people think you're crazy for doing what God tells you to do.

I wasn't sure about all the Sonship stuff, but I was sure that God had put this together. I needed to know that because I am probably one of the worst skeptics you've ever met in your life, especially when I get around different ministries and all their gimmicks. I can tell you Jack Taylor is no ministry gimmick: he's the real deal. He has the integrity of my father, the intelligence of my oldest son, the swagger of John Wayne, and the love of God the Father.

I didn't understand this "spiritual fathering" thing. I didn't know how often I could call; I didn't know when I could call; I didn't know if I only brought praise reports or real-life struggles. Jack told me that I could have all of him that I wanted, but I didn't know what that meant. (He has never told anyone else that since.) We started building a relationship over the cell phone first.

I continued on my trip and arrived at my sister's house in New York on Monday afternoon, August 17, 2010. I slept awhile, got up, and started reading a book about Ivan Q. Spencer. He is one of the fathers of our faith. He founded a Bible school in upstate New York that has sent trained pastors and thousands of missionaries all over the world. From the 1930s until the 1950s, he had a Bible school in Hornell that moved up to Lima, New York, near Rochester, after his son took over.

That night, as I read the autobiography of Ivan Q. Spencer, the Lord spoke to me. "You know I work in forty-year cycles. Would you like a piece of the mantle that Ivan Q. Spencer carried while on earth?"

"Absolutely! He is one of the fathers of the faithful, a true hero in my book."

At that moment, a huge angel appeared in the room, and the whole atmosphere became electric; I heard the voice of my King say, "Turn to the next page and receive what I have for you." On the next page was

Church Fathers vs Kingdom Sons

written, "August 17th, 1970 Ivan Q. Spencer died," exactly forty years to the day from when I was reading it.

I believe many mantles of church fathers have not been picked up and are available for those who are hungry, thirsty, and willing to pay the price for them. You can ask God to give you what you need to be successful in the areas where you've asked for responsibility, in order to expand the kingdom.

Kingdom Key: You can't have what you don't honor.

Learning More about the Bastard Curse

That weekend I preached for Brother Paul at Living Waters Church in Hornell. Sunday was a good meeting. On Monday morning, I was headed to his office to talk to him and his wife. As I pulled into the parking lot, Papa Jack Taylor called me and said it was time for me to receive a father's blessing. He proceeded to pray and pronounce a blessing over my life. Now I'm accustomed to the anointing, but this time I felt it come upon my life from the inside. I felt warmth come all the way out to my fingertips. The big difference about this anointing is that it has never left. It is the anointing of Sonship. It came from the inside, and became a new normal. Some of the insecurities I had, vanished that day. There was a completely new normal; I can still feel it in my hands today.

As I met with Brother Paul, we began to discuss one of his children who had made some bad choices, including fathering a child out of wedlock. He was disgusted and used words that cursed his son. So I challenged him and said, "Listen. I have two sons, and they don't always do what's right, but I don't curse them."

He started to get upset with me, quoting Scriptures and telling me what the Bible says about all that religious crap. All of a sudden I pointed

Round 13: You Don't Know Jack, Until You Know Jack

at him and yelled, "He only reproduced what you are." To my surprise, he said, "How did you know I was a bastard?" I said, "I didn't, but that sure does explain a lot."

We had a time of repentance and deliverance, and we broke some of those things off of his life. Brother Paul is now in his mid-sixties with a PhD, had been in ministry for over forty years, and had literally put hundreds of people in ministry through training schools—all while carrying this lifelong curse.

The "bastard curse" affects so many people that I want to address it now. Take a look at Malachi 4:4–6 (NIV): "Remember the law of my servant Moses, the decrees and laws I gave him at Horeb for all Israel. See, I will send you the prophet Elijah before that great and dreadful day of the Lord comes. He will turn the hearts of the fathers to their children, and the hearts of the children to their fathers; or else I will come and strike the land with a curse."

These are the last few verses of the Old Testament. God is saying He was going to send the prophet Elijah. With the anointing of a prophet, He would turn the hearts of the father to the children, and turn the hearts of the children to the father. This was the antidote needed to remove a curse from the land. You ask, "What kind of curse?" I believe He was talking about a bastard curse.

There was no voice from heaven between the Old Testament and the New Testament. The time between the two testaments was 400 years. Since forty years is a generation, it means the ten generations imposed by a bastard curse is fulfilled. Israel had rejected God as their Father and wanted kings like the other nations. The condition of the family and land was the byproduct:

> A bastard shall not enter into the congregation of the Lord; even to his tenth generation shall he not enter into the congregation of the Lord (Deuteronomy 23:2 KJV).

Church Fathers vs Kingdom Sons

If you are conceived outside of a marriage covenant, you can't find your true spiritual inheritance.

That's why the marriage covenant between you and Jesus in the born-again experience is the only way to the Father.

When the New Testament begins 400 years later, we read the story about God the Father's only begotten Son, Jesus. So, the first voice from heaven in over 400 years is from God, but He starts speaking in the language of the Son. I believe the Sonship message and the father-son paradigm will bring the American church back to wholeness as a family, and then—as families—we'll remove the curse off of our land.

Looking at America today, we are a fatherless generation. We have a fatherless generation with many being conceived outside of a marriage covenant in the natural. We can set this generation free from the curse and bring restoration by getting the children to forgive and bless those very fathers who facilitated the curse. Then this will be the first generation that will have a legal right to a double-portion inheritance. There's no greater time for God to release the Sonship message than now!

Martin Luther had brought his own fight to the Roman Catholic Church, and approximately 400 years later, Father visited us again at Azusa Street in 1906. At Azusa Street the *shekinah* glory cloud of God was so thick that the children would play hide-and-seek in the glory. (Now that's the children's program I want in my church!) William J. Seymour, the founder of the Azusa Street revival, gave a prophecy that 100 years from that time, there would be a move of the glory one more time. It's time for the Father to visit again and heal his church.

Mantles Falling

I gave an altar call at my church one Sunday for the bastard curse and those who had been abandoned or orphaned. After we applied the blood for forgiveness, I started to have them follow me in a prayer. I asked them to forgive their birth parents for what they had done, bless them, and ask for an inheritance from their bloodline. As we did this,

Round 13: You Don't Know Jack, Until You Know Jack

the Spirit showed a mantle of blessing falling on the right shoulder of Hannah, one of my leaders. I had her forgive her adopted parents for any sins she held against them, to bless them, and to ask for their inheritance.

As I looked in the Spirit, I saw a second mantle fall on Hannah's left shoulder. Seeing these two mantles resting on her shoulders, I started to prophesy: "Satan has overplayed his hand one more time! If he had known what the final results of Calvary would be, he would have never crucified Me. He has done it again. He has overplayed his hand and succeeded in making a fatherless generation like never seen on earth. But I will release the Father's love to the fatherless, abandoned, and rejected generation and heal them. They will be the first generation with a legal right to a double portion and will become an army of harvesters."

> Never pay back one wrong with another, or an angry word with another one: instead, payback with a blessing. This is what you are called to do, so that you inherit a blessing yourself (1 Peter 3:9 The Jerusalem Bible).

This revelation of Sonship will release the former orphans to father the fathers. I believe this is the eleventh-hour worker in Matthew 20 with the legal right to a double portion. And what Satan has tried to use as evil, God is going to use as a blessing.

After a time of prayer, Brother Paul looked at me and asked, "Why do you keep coming to New York?"

I said, "Because sixteen years ago, God showed me the wells of revival that have been capped in this city, dating back to the 1830s revival of Charles Finney. God said that He would give me a key that would unlock those wells and that this city would see revival one more time. In the 1930s and '40s, flowing through the Bible school that Ivan Q. Spencer founded, there was a tremendous move of God in this city. My mother actually got saved at one of their camp meetings, so I personally have a little skin in the game here. But after they left, the city became very corrupt financially and morally dark. When spiritual leadership leaves a city or a region, there is usually a vacuum for either godly leadership to emerge and replace them, or for the enemy to take over that place of authority."

Brother Paul said, "I know that when the spiritual leadership of this school left the city, there were broken covenants and relationships within God's people. Now I see that it has been an open door for the enemy to bring destruction, poverty, and moral decay to the city." I asked him to explain further in detail, and here's what he told me: "There was a young girl who had an adulterous relationship with one of the students of the Bible school and became pregnant. Her family was in the leadership of this ministry. When the situation became public, they were asked to remove themselves, and therefore covenants were broken and a spiritual vacuum was left in this city."

I asked him, "How do you know this information?"

He answered, "I am the bastard product of that relationship."

God had just handed us some keys to unlock the old wells of revival. We started repenting for relationships, which had been broken over sixty years before, in the city where we both have responsibility.

Expansion and Unraveling

As I continued to travel to New York, God expanded my territory southward toward Pennsylvania. God showed me an hourglass, which started in Buffalo, went east to Syracuse, and then south down to Hornell with the point down. He added a triangle with the point up, points touching each other in Hornell with the base south all the way to I-80 in Pennsylvania. The Lord told me to make a commitment to network with as many ministries and churches as I could and to bring enough unity to have a move of the Spirit. God used some old relationships to expand influence into Pennsylvania and made some very strong relationships with businesspeople who have a huge vision for the kingdom and are implementing it within their businesses and communities.

Round 13: You Don't Know Jack, Until You Know Jack

I was just starting this new relationship of Sonship with Jack Taylor; my whole paradigm of the gospel was shifting, and a new realm of the kingdom was starting to unfold before my very eyes.

I spent much of 2010 and 2011 in New York and most of the time didn't meet my expenses, which had never been a problem in the past. But I had closed my business, and this was now our livelihood. It's amazing how that will influence what you say from the pulpit … when you need an offering to survive, you have a tendency to be a little nicer.

I was spending most of my time in New York, and because of my absence, my church in Florida was coming apart; I started to feel like a guest speaker there. During this time, the apostolic calling of birthing churches and covering them in relationship was becoming a reality in my spirit; I would come back from a ministry trip with a fresh revelation and the zeal of a traveling evangelist, yet I couldn't make my own church function properly. At this point, I realized that the way it was working, I could not do both.

Rodger and I had reached an impasse in our relationship, and we both knew we were in trouble. We had a confrontation one day when Rodger came to me and told me that, for the first time ever, our vision was no longer the same; he was pretty much accusing me of changing my vision for One Kingdom and our partnership. The vision hadn't changed, but my understanding of how the vision was to be facilitated had begun to evolve. But with the accusation came a heated discussion: a boxing match.

I called him on the carpet and told him he was unwilling to confront and solve situations in his own life and his family. He was unwilling to pay the price and deal with the issues that were holding him back from his true destiny. I yelled at him, letting him know that he wasn't man enough to admit it. When I pointed out that he was actually the one who had completely lost his sense of purpose, he needed to accuse me to take the heat away from himself. This was probably only the third time that Rodger and I had been this vocal and angry at each other in over eighteen years; there's never been a man I've loved more than Rodger. I remember pointing at him and saying, "You lost your vision, and you want to blame me!"

Church Fathers vs Kingdom Sons

At the end of our argument, he said to me he knew the calling on my life. He told God if he was going to be a hindrance, he would back away. We hugged, kissed, and made up, and he left the office.

About three hours later I got a phone call from Rodger's wife. Rodger had been rushed to the hospital, his retina detached in his left eye. I immediately asked God to forgive me if I had any part to play in this situation. At that point we should've come to the conclusion that we were in trouble. But we had both avoided dealing with what was wrong in our relationship, even while knowing that we were in trouble. Our church was suffering. Some people who were close to us both knew that we were in trouble, but neither one of us would man up and deal with our issues. Rodger and I both had been orphans for so long, we did not know how to address the root issues in both of our lives.

Inward Focus

Jack Taylor was beginning to unlock my whole understanding of Sonship, a transformation that I never knew existed. One truth that I witnessed about Jack that was different from all the other systems is openness. On three different occasions Jack asked me to pray for him and father him in a few areas where he felt I had insight. I had never had that before from any leader. But Jack believes that we all can father each other with our strengths.

I have personally watched Jack ask a man to father him. When this happened, I asked the Lord, "What did I just witness?" The Lord answered, "It is the key to kingdom success in fathering."

Kingdom Key: If you will focus on your own Sonship, your fathering will be empowered from Heaven.

I explained to the church body that I had a spiritual father named Jack Taylor. The desperate longing in my heart for approval and

Round 13: You Don't Know Jack, Until You Know Jack

acceptance, along with some of the broken places in my emotions, were being healed. A group of members challenged me, believing that the Bible says that we are not permitted to call anyone "father" but God, challenging my relationship with Papa Jack. They were so dogmatic about it they left our church. I showed them in Scripture where the apostle John often addressed people in this way in his letters: "To my little children." Looks like he thought he was their father! The apostle Paul talks about his sons Timothy and Titus too. It's a theme that runs all through Scripture.

By the way, God the Father spoke audibly from heaven at Jesus's baptism and said, "This is my Son, in whom I am well pleased." Look: Heaven is a mirror of what is to be done in earth. God is a Father, and I was finally starting to see Him in that image.

The first thing I wanted to do was get Jack Taylor to my church, because One Kingdom was hurting. I was hoping Jack would come and bring some unity. He was a true father to me, and I was hoping that the healing I had begun to feel would come to our church body as well.

I actually booked the date for Jack to come. After I booked the date, and as I was praying one morning, the Holy Spirit asked me why I hadn't asked Him if it was okay for Jack Taylor to come preach at my church.

I had no clue that God would not approve of my new spiritual father preaching at my church. Then the Lord spoke clearly, "If you bring Jack Taylor into your fellowship, it will drive a wedge between you and Rodger, and you two will never recover." He told me to call a friend of mine, Louis DeSiena in Jacksonville, and use that particular date for Jack to come up to his place. Jack was there for those dates, and Louis and his wife, Gloria, became spiritual sons of Jack too.

The weekend Jack Taylor and his son Tim went to speak at Louis's church, The Gate Fellowship in Jacksonville, I decided to get a hotel so we could all be together for the weekend. After that weekend with Tim and Jack, I realized that Jack had truly given me a place to sit at the table beside his natural son and I actually had a place where my opinion mattered.

We planned a meeting in Firecreek, located in the mountains outside of Asheville, North Carolina. Jack started to have Sons Gatherings there, and I was at the first one. It's a great place to share some family time! Firecreek is located in the Blue Ridge Mountains. There are three rustic homes hidden in a bowl-shaped area with a pond in the middle. The main house has a big wraparound deck with a fireplace on it. The view alone is spectacular. In addition, Firecreek is a beautiful spot to hold meetings because there are heavenly portals all over the land. Someone has redeemed the land, as we are told to do in Joel 2:18: "Then the Lord will be zealous for His land, and pity His people."

If the robe I wear, combined with my righteousness, can turn filthy lucre into kingdom cash, we can surely restore the land that God loves so much!

I have been to three Firecreek gatherings so far. The first time, I was still trying to figure out this "Sons" thing and whether I had a place at the table or not. We sat around, built relationships, and told our stories. So I put it to the test, and became the open book that I am: porn, rape, guns, and wanting kill things that piss me off. I was definitely trying to test this and make sure I truly had a place at Dad's table.

The second time was a true blessing. Some relationships that were shaky and uncertain from the first time with some of my brothers started to warm up a little, and a true family dynamic began to emerge. If I have a father, then I have brothers. God is very serious about this family of His.

The third trip to Firecreek was the charm: relationships were sealed at this time. It changed me so much I will make my sons or anyone that I have influence with to commit to at least two or three gatherings to get the full picture. And some have balked at this kind of commitment. These are the same people who complain about the people who come to their church a few times a year and don't get involved in real church

Round 13: You Don't Know Jack, Until You Know Jack

family. (Now that I have a little healing, orphans tick me off.) You should have seen me when I stopped smoking! LOL.

Rocky Relationships

I started planning a way to make sure that I got Rodger around Papa Jack. Seven years ago, when I opened my lighting store in Vero Beach, I started a Bible study. I still go every couple of weeks on Wednesday morning at 8:00 a.m., which means I have to leave my house by 5:30 a.m. to get there. Rodger and I would go to the Bible study with the businessmen in Vero Beach and then spend the afternoon with Papa Jack. I did my very best to not interfere with Jack and Rodger's relationship, so that it could be between them, and that he could get the healing that he needed. You can only bring a horse to water, but you cannot make him drink.

About this time Randy came back from China. We sat on my back porch chatting, and he asked what had happened to me. He told me that whatever I had gotten from God, he wanted some of it. That day I prayed a father's blessing over Randy. The anointing was tangible to him, as much as it has been to me. Randy and I have been friends a long time, but we had no clue how this was going to work. We will have to explain in a different book how this father-son relationship works with two very strong prophets. That is a boxing match all by itself. But we made it happen. Randy moved to New York after he came back from China.

There was a shift going on. My understanding about this Sonship stuff and the message I have been carrying for years about how to redeem the land were starting to blend. But in the process, it seemed that all my relationships were falling apart.

I was in New York and was asked to come to a meeting with some leaders of a ministry. A snowstorm hit that day. I was convinced that God had told me to go, so I went without Brother Paul. It should have been a sign that when a local New Yorker won't travel on the roads, a Florida-born redneck shouldn't either.

The meeting could not have gone worse. I wept through most of it. I was being accused of trying to expand my ministry at the expense of their reputations and was asked to never mention their names within my circles of influence.

Fishing with Jesus

This was extremely hurtful for me. I asked God, "What is going on with my ministry? If I keep doing it this way, I will not be successful."

The Lord started to tell me that He was proud of me, continually bringing fresh oil to others with the revelations He was showing me. He then said that not everybody wants to restore inheritances. It's a dirty job cleaning out the old, capped wells; they are full of snakes and rocks. Most people don't have the spiritual guts to deal with the all the crap that needs to be repented for. As I was driving back to Hornell in the worst snowstorm I have ever seen, the Lord told me that because of my obedience, I had gained favor with Him, but I had not yet gained favor with man.

> And Jesus increased in wisdom and stature, and in favor with God and men (Luke 2:52).

He then told me that He would settle this for me in a prophetic dream that night. I was not to be worried about the religious people who rejected me.

When I went to bed the Lord told me He was very pleased with how I was handling all that was going on.

I had a vividly colored dream. I saw a 65-foot Hatteras fishing yacht with outriggers open. We were in the darkest blue waters I have ever seen, and Jesus was standing in the cockpit fishing. As I watched Jesus was catching sailfish, white marlin, and blue marlin. They were all billfish. I saw Him catch about forty different fish. Armed with a yellowish gold glove on his left hand, He dragged each fish by the bill

Round 13: You Don't Know Jack, Until You Know Jack

up so he could whisper in the fish's ear: "Are you going to straighten up and fly right, or do I have to filet you?" With over half the fish, He would take the knife He had in His right hand, cut their throats, and then put them in the fish box. The others He would release from the hook. As He released them, they would do a tail walk across the blue ocean water with what looked like joy because of their freedom. It was beautiful to watch. Jesus looked up and over His right shoulder, gazed directly into my eyes and deep into my soul, and started thanking me for taking Him fishing. He just kept telling me how much He loved to fish and thanked me.

I woke up and told Jesus, "I don't have a sport fishing boat anymore." I used to, but I couldn't see why He was thanking me for taking Him fishing now. Then the Lord said, "Oh, you didn't see the bait I was using." With that I went into a vision. Jesus was back in the boat, showing me that I was the bait. He was thanking me for taking Him fishing because He loves to catch fish. He looked into my eyes and said, "I know it hurts when they bite, but they are the ones I am trying to hook, so I can heal them. Thanks for taking me fishing."

***

Kingdom Keys:

1. If you will focus on your own Sonship, your fathering will be empowered from heaven.
2. Jesus is a fisher of men. Are you mature enough for Him to use you as bait?

Round 14

Multiplication by Death!

> Verily, verily, I say unto you, except a corn of wheat fall into the ground and die, it abideth alone: but if it die, it bringeth forth much fruit (John 12:24 KJV).

In November 2011 I held a leadership meeting with all five of my leaders. At this meeting, I offered three options:

Option number one: I would give Rodger my 501(c)(3) and all of the assets of the church. I would walk away and do nothing but itinerant ministry.

Option two: Rodger would give me complete control and walk away.

Option three: I would take the senior leadership position privately and publicly. Rodger would agree to that, and we would work out our differences and make this thing work.

I gave all five of the leaders a forty-day window to make this decision. I told them I would honor and respect whatever decision they made. I stated that we should have done this eighteen months ago, and that Rodger and I were not even friends now even though we were still friendly. One of the leaders looked to Rodger and asked, "Is this true?" "Yes." He totally agreed this was no longer working. I was going to a conference in Seattle, and when I returned, they could tell me what they had decided.

Church Fathers vs Kingdom Sons

Well, no one made a decision within the forty-day window. Fifty-two days later, God invaded my bedroom in the morning. He was not sweet baby Jesus lying in a manger. God was angry with me! The Lord told me that I had jeopardized my own calling because of my love for Rodger and my lack of obedience to Him. I was sternly warned that if Rodger and I did not separate now, there would never be an opportunity to reconnect properly in the future. With that I called Rodger, weeping, and told him what the Lord said. Three days later, he called me back and agreed it was time.

Our first reaction was to just close the church. It was struggling financially and, truthfully, had become a royal pain. I was still having success with my Thursday night Bible studies, and I had many spiritual sons traveling from as far as Orlando. In my scramble to figure out what to do, we had a meeting with the leadership. At that time, all of them checked out and were leaving One Kingdom except Simon.

Here I was yet again, having to make the hard decisions alone. It appeared as if One Kingdom Fellowship was coming to an end, but I knew that I still needed to teach on Thursday evenings. I called Pastor George Jones.

A Mother's Touch

The Thursday morning between Christmas and New Year's was heartbreaking for me. I had lost every one, and I was hurting deep inside. As I prayed that morning, I could not voice what I needed from the Lord and felt lower than whale's poop. On the way to work I started telling God that I wanted my mom. She always made things better. When I was seven and God told her to rock me to sleep every night, she would prophesy over me and tell me Bible stories. My mother believed in me when no one else did.

As I arrived at the church and slipped into my office that morning, I felt an anointing enter the room. Out of the corner of my eye, I saw a figure dressed in a white linen robe walk into my office. For some

Round 14: Multiplication by Death!

reason, I couldn't look at the face. I asked, "Is that You, Jesus?" He answered no, then asked, "Who were you asking for?"

"My mother."

I looked at my mother's hand and it was not crippled any more. This was a different encounter than I have had before. I asked the Lord about this, and He said, "Heaven is starting to invade the earth realm." I called Susie and explained what had just happened. I told her that the moment Mom came in, I knew that everything was going to be all right. She was one of the saints, dressed in white linen, part of the great cloud of witnesses interceding for my inheritance to be fulfilled on the earth. Then Susie and I prayed together.

At six o'clock, Hannah came to the church early for Bible study and wanted to see me. She asked me not to make fun of her, but she believed the Lord told her to demonstrate a prophetic act. She pulled up a chair and made me sit in her lap. She felt she represented my mother and that everything was going to be all right. Susie walked through the door while I was crying on Hannah's lap and assumed I had told Hannah about what had happened that day. But I had not. Hannah had no clue about her prophecy. I have no doubt that God is releasing all heaven for our benefit to redeem our inheritance.

Double Blessing

I went to the breakfast meeting the next day that had been setup with Pastor George and asked him if he could help meet some of my needs. I was hoping to use his facility on Tuesday nights to rebuild the leadership and on Thursday nights for a Bible study. As I laid out my plans, Pastor George totally agreed, with no hesitation, and made it extremely affordable.

When I was finished, George looked at me and asked, "Is that all you wanted?" I said, "Yes."

Church Fathers vs Kingdom Sons

George asked me if the Lord had shown me anything about him and his wife doing ministry with me. To my amazement, he shared that he and Judy had known for years that they were supposed to be submitted to me in ministry. He proposed blending the two churches under my leadership, submitted to me as the apostle and a senior leader. It could prove to be a double blessing, since Judy is probably the best children's minister in the county: they were willing to submit and be my associates if I would have them. The Lord reminded me of the dream that Rodger's wife had had. And here both of them were, willing to come and to fill those roles that the church desperately needed.

Only God could bring these kinds of things together. There was definite room for bitterness between us. At one time they had been my pastors, but I wound up with a financial blessing in a building that they chose to leave. However, they still had the ability to hear God and try to follow him. With lots of decisions to be made on all sides, it was a crazy Christmas season for all of us. There were lots of options and no concrete decisions had been made yet.

Two Triangles Merging

There I was on January 2, standing out in front of the church, looking at a building I could not afford and asking God what to do.

The Holy Spirit bellowed at me, and here's what He said: "I finally have you right where I want you—by yourself, completely surrendered to me. You have no one to turn to, and that is by My design. You made covenants with people to cover your weaknesses. You made covenants that usurped the covenant with your wife. You've been bellyaching, whining for her to stand up and to take her rightful place, but you never made room for her because of covenants that you had made with others. You need to break all of them and make room for her to stand beside you and lead this ministry as a team."

He gave me instructions on how to deal with the landlord. He showed me two triangles and told me that George and Judy's church

Round 14: Multiplication by Death!

was one triangle and the remnant of One Kingdom Fellowship was the other triangle, and He was going to give me the grace to blend the two. I'd like to tell you that we didn't lose any people, but we did. Everyone's wagon got turned upside down.

Simon was the remaining leader who didn't walk out. But when he heard that George and Judy were going to join us, he demonically manifested. He started cussing me out on the phone: "So, when you're preaching in New York, who is going to be in charge?" He wigged out and temporarily lost his mind. Simon spent a few years in prison because of this kind of behavior, and I had had enough. Simon demanded, "Who is going to be in charge, me or George?" He started all this "I have been faithful" crap. So I finished cleaning house with Simon.

It was official: I was totally leaderless. Only me. I was all alone. About ninety minutes later, Simon called back like always and repented. I thought I was done, but the Lord told me this would bring a healing that would last. It had better, because I was ticked off.

The next day, Simon came to the church and we talked. He started repenting to me, and confessed how bad he felt for the way he cussed me. He still tried to justify himself because I was his spiritual father, and it hurt and made him angry that George would be in charge and he was being overlooked.

I asked, "What did your father do to you at four years old?"

He said, "I love my dad."

I asked, "What did he do to you at four years old?"

"I love my dad."

"Simon!"

He started yelling: "I hate my father! I hate my father! But I want to love him. I led him to the Lord before he died."

Church Fathers vs Kingdom Sons

I saw a large angel holding a yellow cordless screw gun. Attached to it was a 36-inch metal shaft with clawlike barbs on it. (You've seen the TV ad to remove weeds in the garden.) He pushed it into Simon's chest. We heard the most grueling screams when the angel pulled out this demon that had been in Simon's heart since he was four years old.

As I started to pray, Simon and I both saw a man dressed in white linen enter the room. I asked, "Jesus, is that You?" He said, "No, it's Simon's father. He has been trading on the trading floors of heaven for Simon's deliverance and is now here to bless him with a father's blessing."

This encounter has changed both Simon's life and mine. God is doing some great things!

I can tell you that blending two systems together is not easy. I had a group of people who have walked with me, some of them for almost four years, and they understood the kingdom lifestyle that I taught. Now we had another group of people who were entrenched in church doctrine and, while very good at keeping the anointing in the church, were pretty much clueless about how the kingdom functions. So the kingdom thinkers who thought they were real spiritual got upset that I would give a place to the old religious system, and they became meaner than the old church system people.

I felt like I was in the middle of an Old West shootout. One triangle was shooting at the other one, and both were standing on what they claimed were biblical principles. The church people claimed that I had no structure, wouldn't exercise authority, and forced people to submit and behave themselves. The super-spiritual kingdom group would whisper that I really didn't understand the kingdom as much as I claimed to. I would overhear in the spirit realm that all my wounding had blinded my revelation.

At this point, I asked God for permission to kill everyone and let me throw in the towel! Instead, He used it as a great teaching tool for me. The Lord told me to explain to those who would listen that in the Spirit, these thoughts, attitudes, and influences were word curses. The curses came in the form of arrows and were penetrating the hearts of the brothers and

Round 14: Multiplication by Death!

sisters in the body. Now, this wasn't some demonic activity from the outside. These were Christian word curses coming from the inside. One triangle system was shooting at the other triangle system, and both claimed to have the word of the Lord and the authority to stand and exercise judgment. (And if we're not careful, all of us get caught up and do this.)

It became obvious that George and Judy felt like they did not fit into our system whatsoever. They were prepared to leave. This was a tough season for me, because I had sworn that I would not tolerate what had happened in the last season. I would deal quickly with issues and not let them fester, like I had in the past. But the Holy Spirit told me to be quiet. He showed me that some of the leadership, who had come over with George and Judy, had picked up the kingdom message.

One of their leaders received the kingdom principles. When he informed me that George and Judy were planning to leave, God told me to tell them to help solve the problem because of his long relationship with George and Judy. I told him that I was prepared to be thrown under the bus and be the scapegoat if it was necessary, but I wanted to try and bring healing to them at all costs and let them know that God chose them. I did not choose them. He was to reinforce the fact that I loved them and believed that God was in the middle of this merger. This leader was amazed at my willingness to be wrong so others could get right. We all eventually were able to sit down and work out our hurts and wounds and frustrations.

Kingdom Key: In the church, people model what you do. But in the kingdom, you reproduce who you are.

Finding the Right Place

After this crisis, the Lord spoke to me and said, "I told you to make covenant with them. Explain your value of covenant to them and tell them that the covenant has now been tested." Now let us find our rightful places in the kingdom and build this church properly.

I desperately needed George and Judy's gifting, but in this area of my own Sonship and understanding I was no longer going to jeopardize my role as the senior leader. As I finish writing this chapter, we are about to celebrate our one-year anniversary together.

In the midst of this crisis, I truly had come to the end of my rope. I was sitting in my office at the church, where a picture of the triangle-up system and a picture of the triangle-down system hangs on one wall, and on the front wall of my office I have a picture of the Star of David with Jesus in the middle.

In Genesis 25:21–24, we read:

> Now Isaac pleaded with the Lord for his wife, because she was barren: and the Lord granted his plea, and Rebekah his wife conceived. But the children struggled together within her: and she said, if all is well why am I like this? So she went to inquire of the Lord. And the Lord said to her: "Two nations are in your womb, two people shall be separate from your body: one people shall be stronger than the other, and the older shall serve the younger." So when her days were fulfilled for her to give birth, indeed there were twins in her womb.

As the Lord started revealing to me what the Scriptures were saying, He showed me that Rebekah had been barren for over twenty years. I am just now coming into my twentieth year of serving the Lord Jesus Christ. But Isaac prayed for Rebekah, and she finally conceived. She thought that her days of rejection from the Lord were over, since in that culture once you conceived all was supposed to be well. Like Rebekah, I know I have been pregnant with a promise and a blueprint from heaven, but there's been a boxing match going on inside of my spiritual womb, just like hers. When she inquired of the Lord, she was told by Him to

Round 14: Multiplication by Death!

endure the boxing match going on inside and that the older would serve the younger.

As I sat and pondered, "What are you showing me?" Jesus came to me and visited me with tears in His eyes. He said, "Charlie, please do not abort the babies that you're carrying." I pleaded with the Lord for some supernatural prenatal care, because it felt like I was trying to birth two rhinoceroses backward. Then I felt the grace of His love totally engulf me.

The boxing match has been both painful and beneficial, but I believe that we are on the right road for both systems to function together. I think that the older system of the church will become a foundation for the kingdom to manifest God's glory. The Lord's Prayer says it best: "Our Father who art in heaven, hallowed be thy name. Thy kingdom come. Thy will be done, on earth as it is in heaven."

How can we bring heaven to earth when we do not know how to operate in the heavenly realms? Authority in the heavenly realms is through Sonship, not just with an earthly father like Papa Jack, or by becoming spiritual fathers. We gain authority by going into the heavenly kingdom. Our rightful inheritance is seeing Papa God face-to-face. Under the law, you couldn't see God face-to-face; but under grace, we can.

Kingdom Key: Grace is to be a positive empowerment for righteousness, not a defensive excuse for sin.

Kingdom Keys:

1. In the church, people model what you do. But in the kingdom, people reproduce who you are.

Church Fathers vs Kingdom Sons

2. Under the law, man and God never meet face-to-face, but in the kingdom they do.
3. Because of the cross of Jesus Christ, there is no greater sin than to commit the sin that was committed against you.
4. Grace is to be a positive empowerment for righteousness, not a defensive excuse for sin.

Round 15

Bringing Heaven to Earth

I thoroughly enjoy the revelation of Sonship and my relationship with my spiritual father, Jack Taylor. God has used this revelation to release fresh anointing and healing within my life. I'm sure that many have felt as if I have become a fanatic over this message of Sonship. But like Mary who wiped Jesus's feet with her tears because she was so happy to have her sins forgiven, so I, too, have rejoiced in, promoted, and reproduced what Papa Jack has given me.

I now have personal sons and daughter-sons who are finding the healing that I have and are starting to walk out their relationship with God at a much deeper level.

In my pursuit of revival, I found God as a Father!

Spiritual Sons Gather

As I started to walk in my own Sonship, God revealed to others that I was a spiritual father. It's like a neon sign over my head got turned on that read, "Father—Open for Business."

One night, Ron, an eighty-four-year-old who had been coming to my Thursday night Bible study, came up to me after the meeting and handed me a note asking if I would be his spiritual father. He said that he had been looking for me for over sixty-eight years. I have several sons from that generation who have never been spiritually fathered.

Church Fathers vs Kingdom Sons

I have found in the church system that the fathers choose the sons, and then in most cases mold then to look and act just like them. I believe that in the kingdom, the sons will pick the fathers as the Spirit highlights them. Ladies, you are sons. If I can be part of the bride, you can be sons in the kingdom.

Women in the Kingdom

Coming to terms with the roles women play in ministry today has been a growth process for me. I had to undo quite a bit of religious teaching; I was taught that women could not be preachers, much less apostles. It was a life-changing experience when I had to buy an army jacket for $125 and then put five stars on it, give it to a female leader, and publicly declare she was an apostle. After I allowed this revelation to change my ability to help fulfill their destinies, I have seen that gifting on many women. I have always believed that the role of the apostle is the fathering gift of the fivefold ministry.

One time I was in New York doing some regional meetings when I prophesied over a woman. I was sure I could see the ministry gift of the apostle on her life and was speaking about what I saw. The Lord showed me that she had gone even deeper in the process of the kingdom. He showed me that she had a set of spiritual testicles. Her true calling was the ability to reproduce the kingdom as a spiritual father, and this would develop as she pursued Sonship. This revelation has come through the process of seeing the Lord's army of women who will be instrumental in this revival and great harvest.

Some of Satan's twisted attacks on women in ministry have been over the ability to reproduce with seed. In Genesis 3:15, God said that the seed of the woman would bruise the head of Satan. The kingdom seed that a woman has is the prophetic gifting of the word of God. In the kingdom, women have spiritual seed just like the men do, so fathering is not a male gender club in the kingdom. Too many woman have had to fight for their rightful place in the body, but if they stop after they are

Round 15: Bringing Heaven to Earth

confirmed as apostles and don't complete the journey to Sonship, they will build a ministry on their gifting and not the kingdom family.

When we wear the robe of Sonship that Jesus gives us, we position ourselves to also become spiritual fathers, both male and female.

Kingdom Fathering

I asked the Lord, "How do I keep this father-son relationship pure and not create a network or create another 'ism' worse than denominationalism?" He told me that if I have as many sons from outside my church as within, I would stay balanced. This is not building a mountain to me, and it will keep me pure with true kingdom DNA.

With that formula, God spoke to me about my spiritual son, Brad, and showed me that I had brought a lot of healing to him. He said to go speak to Apostle Fowler in Orlando, and send Brad and Earl off to serve him in his church. This is kingdom fathering. I had taken Brad as far as my personal gifting could take him, so although I am still fathering Brad, he is serving under Apostle Fowler.

> **Kingdom Key: If people are your greatest asset, what better seed to sow for a greater harvest?**

A CEO or a director of an orphanage usually would never send a strong leader who is faithful and a good tither to someone else. (Why is it always the good givers?) But a generous father will release a son to complete training that is required to be successful in the kingdom. You can only reproduce who you are, so that puts God back in the driver's seat and keeps this father-son paradigm pure.

A little over a year ago, I took a road trip and went to several of my cousins' houses on the East Coast from Florida to New York. One by one, I started sharing the power of the father's blessing with them.

Church Fathers vs Kingdom Sons

Many of us who were raised in church watched our fathers and mothers who were leaders serve God with their whole hearts. But there was something missing in our father's generation. None of us had ever received a father's blessing.

As I finished this trip, I wound up in New York at my sister's house. I called my father and asked, "Dad, how is it that your generation completely missed the power of the father's blessing?"

His answer completely shocked me. He said, "Charlie, some things you have to earn."

I asked, "Dad, what Bible have you been reading?" I told him that was bogus and that a son should never have to earn his father's blessing. I hung up on him and told God I was not going to fight with him any longer about this.

Three weeks later, on a Monday morning, the Holy Spirit told me to call my father and repent for being angry with him. I was in no frame of mind to discuss it any longer with him. I told God that if He couldn't get his attention, I was no longer going to try to deal with him. About two hours later, the Holy Spirit prompted me again: "Call your father to discuss this matter with him." I told God that if He couldn't talk to him, convince him that he was wrong, and to call me, there'd be no call, because I refused to fight with him any longer.

Spiritual Orphan

At about five o'clock that afternoon, I got a phone call from the emergency room of the hospital. My eighty-five-year-old father had been riding his bicycle and was hit by a truck going 55 miles per hour. He was airlifted to the trauma center thirty miles away. I immediately asked the Lord if I had caused the situation. He informed me that I told Him to get my dad's attention, because I refused to deal with him any longer.

Round 15: Bringing Heaven to Earth

I went into a vision and was shown the symbolism of the accident. The Lord told me that he was going to be okay. He would not have any broken bones, and I did not need to go until 3:00 p.m. the next day. As I walked into his hospital room the doctors were just leaving, amazed that he had no broken bones.

I sat down next to my dad and told him that I had a word from the Lord. He interrupted me. "Before you get started, I need to talk to you about the phone call we had a few weeks ago. I've been meaning to call you and tell you that I was wrong." Those are words I'd not heard much from him.

I started talking to him about the prophetic symbols God had shown me about his accident. A large, white, extended-cab truck represented the corporate ministry vehicle. My father and uncles, who were leaders in the past, were riding in it. My father was riding his bicycle, which represents the ministry that he is now doing in the prison systems. When the mirror of the large truck struck him in the back of the head and threw him into the middle of a highway, the paramedics had to cut his clothes off to find the trauma and then airlift him to the hospital for healing. I explained to my dad that the mirror was looking at the history of what had been accomplished in the church system. It threw him into the highway, representing humanity, to expose the wounds of the past system, in which he was a leader.

I told my dad that he needed to choose to help me in ministry and heal the wounds from the system where he used to be a leader. My dad received the revelation and said to me, "Listen, I will do whatever you tell me to do. Just don't get me killed!"

Several months later I spent a weekend with my dad, and when I got home, he called me. He said, "Charlie, you have offended me this weekend."

"How did I offend you this time, Dad?"

"You keep insinuating that I am a spiritual orphan."

Church Fathers vs Kingdom Sons

"Dad," I said, "I want to be extremely blunt with you and tell you this. You are one of the worst spiritual orphans I have ever seen."

His answer shocked me. I expected another round of boxing with him, like I have had most of my life when we talk about revelation about the kingdom. Instead, he said this to me: "Well, when are you going to man up, pray a father's blessing over me, and break this thing off of my life?"

As I prayed a father's blessing over my own father, I felt the heavens themselves begin to open. I don't know if it did anything for him personally at that moment, but the fulfillment of what my mother had told me on her deathbed was starting to come into alignment with the kingdom. Sometimes you don't know what God is doing till you see the results.

Turning the Hearts of the Fathers to the Sons

A week later, while I was in prayer, the Holy Spirit gave me a revelation about Central Assembly in Vero Beach, which had been started from a church split over 40 years ago. I called my Dad with this revelation that God had given me and started to explain it. He stopped me and said this, "Charlie, I don't have a clue what you're trying to show me. But I trust you and I know that it's God. Call Pastor and make an appointment. Tell me where to be, what time to be there, and I'll do whatever you ask me to do."

With that, I called Pastor and made an appointment. My father is the only living deacon who was part of the leadership from over forty years ago; therefore, he carries the legal responsibility of the broken relationships that occurred under their watch.

Many times while cleansing the land in the regions of New York and Florida, I have had to repent for sins that were many generations old; but when my father, still alive, repents and then blesses, it releases a double portion. As I watched these two giants in the kingdom ask not only each other's forgiveness, but also the organizations they represented, I felt the anointing of the Holy Spirit. I had brought a basin of water and a

Round 15: Bringing Heaven to Earth

towel, and my father and I washed his feet together as a father-son team and anointed his feet with perfume. Finally, my father prayed a blessing over him.

Something happened that day in the kingdom that I cannot explain. But when my father got in the car with me, he said to me, "Your mother's prophecy has now been fulfilled. I believe you're a man of God, and I will serve you."

The Lord has shown me that when the generation of a father can submit to the generation of the son, there is a double-portion anointing that comes on them both. The Lord showed me that the body of Christ has been a generation behind the world, as demonstrated by Ishmael and Isaac. Ishmael had twelve sons and became a nation. Isaac had two sons. Jacob, the next generation, had twelve sons and became the nation of Israel. This gap can be overcome by the older generation—while still alive and in her prime—getting underneath the younger generation, blessing them, and submitting to them. The body of Christ can then walk in a double-portion anointing and become the head, not the tail, in all areas of life, not just within the walls of the church building.

The seven mountains of influence on the earth today are there for our taking. If we will operate with kingdom principles, we can have the influence to rule on earth and not only in the heavens.

Those mountains of influence are Media, Government, Education, Economy, Celebration, Religion, and Family.

Kingdom of Earth vs. Kingdom of Heaven

Thus says the Lord of hosts: 'If you will walk in My ways, and if you will keep My command, then you shall also judge My house, and likewise have charge of My courts; I will give you places to walk among these who stand here' (Zechariah 3:7).

I asked God two questions:

Church Fathers vs Kingdom Sons

1. If I am supposed to govern (or judge) the church with kingdom principles on earth, what is Your formula in which I am to function?

2. If I'm supposed to have charge over the courts in heaven, what is the formula, and how do I execute it with the right protocols?

With all the strife and rumbling that went on between the two systems within my own church, God finally gave me the answers to both questions. In a vision, I walked into my office at church and on the credenza behind my desk I had five baseball hats with these names on them: Apostle, Prophet, Evangelist, Pastor, and Teacher. As I walked into my office I saw the five hats. I walked behind my desk and took off my crown of Sonship and placed it on my desk. Then I leaned my King scepter in the corner and removed my priestly robe that I was wearing. I turned, grabbed the five hats, and went out into the main sanctuary. I started teaching the people how to come into the unity of the faith and become mature in their own Sonship and how to function in the kingdom realm as Sons, Kings, and Priests. When we bring the two triangles together properly, we will bring heaven to earth.

All of the struggling and fighting that has taken place has been for one simple reason: I have been fighting for my true inheritance, as we all do.

I finally have the answer about why I never fit in any of the systems or networks where God told me to submit. They were good, and God is using them, but there was never the transference of inheritance of the kingdom DNA that I was looking for.

Ephesians 4:11–13 (emphasis added) holds the key for me:

> And He Himself gave some to be apostles, some prophets, some evangelists, and some pastors and teachers, for the *equipping* of the saints for the work of ministry, for the edifying of the body of Christ, till we all come to the unity of the faith and of the knowledge of the Son of

Round 15: Bringing Heaven to Earth

> God, to a *perfect* man, to the measure of the stature of the fullness of Christ.

The first thing I noticed was that the fivefold ministry is a temporary office of ministry. It will eventually become obsolete, when the body of Christ comes into the fullness of its maturity.

I am not planning to walk through the pearly gates one day, look at God, and say, "Hey, Apostle Charlie is here" or "Prophet Doodad is here." No! I will be introduced as a Son to my heavenly Father. I have come to the conclusion that the same robe that Jesus put on me, the one that has empowered me to live a holy life and given me boldness to exercise authority over my family, is also the robe of Sonship. Jesus was a Priest and a Son, and He carried all fivefold gifts. But He was also a King. I will be wearing my robe of righteousness, which has the dual robe of Sonship.

Let's look at the word "equipping," which is *katartismos* in the Greek. See Strong's #2677: "A making fit, preparing, training, perfecting, making fully qualified for service."

The great physician is now making all the necessary adjustments so the church will not be "out of joint."

Let's look at the word "perfect," *teleio* in the Greek. Strong's #5466 refers to that which has reached an end; that is, finished, complete, and perfect.

When applied to people, it signifies consummate soundness and includes the idea of being whole. More particularly, when applied to believers it denotes maturity. I was created in God's image, which means I was created a "spirit being."

> God is Spirit, and those who worship Him must worship in spirit and truth (John 4:24).

Church Fathers vs Kingdom Sons

In order to enter the kingdom and function as the spiritual son that I am, I have to come to the end of myself, allowing Christ to complete the finished work that He did on the cross, making me whole.

In John 3, Jesus told Nicodemus that he must be born again to see the kingdom. Look at what Jesus *said*, and also what Jesus *did not say*. He said Nicodemus could *see* the kingdom. He did not say that he was *in* the kingdom. It was only available to him if he was willing to pay the price of surrender and to come to the end of himself: spiritual MATURITY. I know a lot of people who are born again but have no clue about the kingdom. It's through the dying of your flesh and the maturing of your understanding that you enter the kingdom and then find your rightful place among those who walk there.

My true inheritance is to function as a Son, a King, and a Priest. A spirit being, within the kingdom realm under these functions, brings heaven to earth. He then uses the fivefold ministry gifts to bring the body of Christ into unity of faith and maturity in their Sonship. We are to model the father-son paradigm as a family, which is a mirror image of the way it is in heaven.

As a Son: To be about the Father's business.

As a King: To take charge of His courts and to judge His house.

As a Priest: To make sure I bring the proper sacrifices through intercession that pleases the Father in both realms, heavenly and earthly.

Passing Down the Inheritance

As I started to be thankful to God for bringing me to maturity, He asked if I trusted Him. (That's not a good sign).

I had proven I was willing to pay whatever price it took to have my inheritance and promises of revival. I had to work through the natural inheritance with my son when I was painting the house that he bought with the money he saved while in Iraq. I was painting alone in the house

Round 15: Bringing Heaven to Earth

and feeling a little sad. I was limited to doing manual labor and couldn't write checks the way I used to.

God spoke and said, "Bryan's blessing is from your inheritance to him. Good job."

I told God, "Thanks, but that doesn't impress me. What about natural inheritance?"

"What would you like to give him as a sign that you're proud of him?" God asked me.

"Lord, he has a new car. He and Lori are married and have a beautiful little girl, Madison. They are blessed. If I had money like I had previously, I would give him a boat to enjoy with his family like we used to."

"Okay, I will handle it," He offered. Then He asked, "If you're so concerned about making sure of the natural inheritance versus spiritual, you know Jason is also living from your blessing. What about him? What do you want him to have?"

I could feel this one coming from the inside. "The Rolex? No, not my Rolex! But God, it was a sign that revival was coming." I then let God know that if He wanted me to give my Rolex to Jason, I would, but to have Susie confirm it.

That night we were talking about ministry in New York, and Susie said, "The Rolex has been a sign to you, but it doesn't mean what it used to. You should give it to Jason. He likes good watches." There's your sign, redneck … Jason took the Rolex and thanked me for it.

The next day, Alex came into the office with a large blue boat bumper that keeps boats from slamming into the dock. He told me that God was about to give me a buffer to help me not to slam into the dock any more. Then he gave me the title to a boat that I had given him several years ago. The Lord told him to sow it back into my life. I was able to give it to Bryan as a gift from me to welcome him home from the army.

Church Fathers vs Kingdom Sons

Man, I wished I had never had this inheritance burden come on me.

Family Meeting Time

I bankrupted my company and gave several buildings back to the bank. I was supposed to retire with millions; now God was telling me to put the New York ministry on the altar. The church was crappy, I had my own boat repossessed, and Jason got my watch. And God asks me, "Do You trust Me?"

"God, I am getting mad! I am calling a family meeting!" I told the Lord, "This sucks! All I get is a stupid promise with a blue boat bumper and a word that You're going to help keep me from slamming into docks. I am getting frustrated with promises. I want my stuff back. God, I feel like a 'dirtball.'"

Then the Holy Spirit reminded me that eighteen years prior, Jason had told me I was turning this family into dirtballs. He started telling me that my family trusted me when they felt like dirtballs, but they followed me as I followed God. Now they have the ability to hear God's voice and have a relationship with Him. He was proud of me and that I was maturing in my walk.

The journey has been hard, but yes, I trust you, PAPA.

Welcome to "begotten Sonship," your true inheritance.

"Jesus, what is begotten Sonship?"

"A son who is ruled by the single thought: 'What does the Father want?' One who is willing to die at the hands of others and walk in love, so that the Father gets the credit."

Father also gets the opportunity to love them instead of giving them what they deserve and to bring healing.

> For God so loved the world that He gave His only *begotten* Son, that whoever believes in Him should not

Round 15: Bringing Heaven to Earth

perish but have everlasting life (John 3:16, emphasis added).

The Greek word for "begotten" is *monogenes*. Per *Strong's*, G3439: "A single gene. Mono- single; Gen- to cause to 'gen'-erate."

The DNA of God is the Christ in you, the hope of glory. When this kingdom seed is the prominent focus, the kingdom of heaven and the kingdom of earth kiss in the form of the Father's love.

I asked the Lord what test I had passed to advance to this level. He said, "Like Abraham, you were willing to sacrifice your promise of revival. I knew I could trust you. Even when others don't agree, you have tried to obey Me. I also love your willingness to take Me fishing and let Me use you as the bait."

This is my Son, in whom I am well pleased.

Let's expand the kingdom!

***

Kingdom Keys:

1. In my pursuit for revival, I found God as a Father!
2. If people are your greatest asset, what better seed to sow for a greater harvest.

Conclusion

The Power of Redeemed Orphans!

"Well-Behaved Women Rarely Make History"

Last year, in obedience to the Lord, I stopped traveling to New York. I have gone through a death process concerning all the promises of revival. But in that process I have found God to be a Father in new and personal ways. My church has also been merging as a family, and new things are happening between Susie and me.

We were blessed with a condo on the beach for a few weeks. During that time I realized I had been promoted in the kingdom. I told Susie things are changing. The night before I had asked God if I had found favor with Him, and if so, man, I wanted a new Rolex. I didn't want the one I had given to Jason. I wanted God to give me a new one, at least a blue-faced Submariner or one of the several others that I like.

A few days later, Jason came up to work on his rental house. He called Susie and told her he had left my Rolex on the dresser. He felt like that was what he was supposed to do. I had wanted a new one, but God showed me how the son was giving his inheritance back to his father. Sounds a lot like family.

A few weeks later I was preparing to go to Louis DeSiena's church in Jacksonville. I asked the Lord, "What am I to preach on, and what am I to bring to their church?" He started to review with me all the

Church Fathers vs Kingdom Sons

different anointings I have carried into a city or church. Sometimes I have brought the prophet, the apostle, or even the evangelist. This time the Lord said, "I have a new mantle of anointing for you to bring to Jacksonville. You are bringing the anointed mantle of a brother. You are the brother of Louis and Gloria, bringing a brother's love to them and the anointing of a rich uncle to their church body." This was a totally new anointing for me, and we had a great meeting. This "family thing" in the kingdom is real.

A few weeks ago I was preaching on God being a Father. I was sharing the fight I had had against my beliefs of how God functions as a father because my experience in the natural was one of living with a strict father who taught that his children had to earn his love. Right in the middle of my message, Susie came and took the microphone. She began to explain how her opinion of God the Father was different from mine. She told the church that when she got pregnant at age sixteen, her father came to her bedside, told her that he was sorry for what had happened to her, and he would stand beside her. He told her that there was nothing she could do that would make him ashamed of her.

She started to tell the congregation that that's how God the Father is. There is nothing that you have done or could do that would make Him ashamed of you. Nothing! The power of God hit the room. Susie laid hands on and prayed for people who came down front for over an hour.

Later that day, as we talked about what happened, Susie said that it's only been the last few years that she believed we serve the same God.

Susie and I serve the same God, but too much of the time I only show one side. God is love, and that has to be the foundation.

When the foundation of love supports the archway of honor, a door of God's favor will open to you.

After twenty years of trying on my own, I believe that I am just now starting to walk in my ministry calling.

Conclusion: The Power of Redeemed Orphans!

Thanks, Mom, for giving a word from God that kept Dad and me in the ring fighting long enough to find the kingdom and the Father.

I was given a word from the Lord: "The assignment of Obadiah has come to an end." He spoke that same word for over a week every morning: "The assignment of Obadiah has come to an end."

I read the whole book of Obadiah a few times, but it meant nothing to me. So I inquired a little more about what God was showing me, and He said Obadiah was the servant of Ahab and Jezebel. See 1 Kings 18:3–4:

> And Ahab had called Obadiah, who was in charge of his house. (Now Obadiah feared the Lord greatly. For so it was, while Jezebel massacred the prophets of the Lord, that Obadiah had taken one hundred prophets and hidden them, fifty to a cave, and had fed them with bread and water.)

The assignment of Obadiah has come to an end. Tell the prophets who are hiding in the caves that it's time to clean up from sloppy cave living and prepare to find their rightful place in the kingdom.

Tell the prophets who are hiding in the caves that it's time to clean up from sloppy cave living and prepare to find their rightful place in the kingdom.

I then saw a vision of a mountain where the prophets were hiding in the very back of the cave, as far away from the opening they could get. I then saw wives, pastors, and Christian leaders trying to drag them back into the church system with words of rebuke, shame, and manipulation. To get away from the old system, they ran to the end of the cave as far as they could get.

Church Fathers vs Kingdom Sons

I was watching this from a viewpoint where I could see the whole mountain. The cave opening was the old church system. On the opposite side was the thin wall of the back of the cave. The Lord spoke to me, "Tell them they will not go back into what was old, but they are to prepare to emerge into the kingdom." Then I saw three angels with C-4 plastic explosive set charges outside on the thin back wall of the mountain. As the explosives detonated, there was an opening for the prophets to emerge into the kingdom.

> For Jesus Himself testified that a prophet has no honor in his own country (John 4:44).

The assignments of Obadiah and Abraham Lincoln have now come to an end. We need to find our rightful places within the kingdom.

Susie has a quote on the fridge that I like: "Well-behaved women rarely make history."

I have always looked to the Bible for my life lessons and have found that God has done some of His best work, many times, with redeemed orphans and slaves.

So, as we look at Scripture, there is no excuse for you or me to remain broken, to not receive the blessing of healing and become whole. We can have a double portion if we're willing to fight for what is rightfully ours. Let's look at Jephthah's journey in Judges 11:1–8:

> Now Jephthah the Gileadite was a mighty man of valor, but he was the son of a harlot; and Gilead begot Jephthah. Gilead's wife bore sons; and when his wife's sons grew up, they drove Jephthah out, and said to him, "You shall have no inheritance in our father's house, for you are the son of another woman." Then Jephthah fled from his brothers and dwelt in the land of Tob; and worthless men banded together with Jephthah and went out raiding with him. It came to pass after a time that the people of Ammon

Conclusion: The Power of Redeemed Orphans!

made war against Israel. And so it was, when the people of Ammon made war against Israel, that the elders of Gilead went to get Jephthah from the land of Tob. Then they said to Jephthah, "Come and be our commander, that we may fight against the people of Ammon." So Jephthah said to the elders of Gilead, "Did you not hate me, and expel me from my father's house? Why have you come to me now when you are in distress?" And the elders of Gilead said to Jephthah, "That is why we have turned again to you now, that you may go with us and fight against the people of Ammon, and be our head over all the inhabitants of Gilead."

Jephthah, a son of a harlot, rejected, and willing to fight for his rightful inheritance, became a captain of the ones who stole his birthright.

Abraham had to leave his father's house and go to a land that God would show him; he had to deal with family issues, and then he had to put his promise on the altar so God would know that he trusted Him.

Moses had to float his assets to be adopted by Pharaoh's daughter. However, when his true inheritance came into view, he reacted with zeal and was banished to the desert for forty years to be de-orphan-ized of his orphan spirit. His wife called him a bloody husband. Ultimately, he got his reward.

> By faith Moses, when he became of age, refused to be called the son of Pharaoh's daughter, choosing rather to suffer affliction with the people of God than to enjoy the passing pleasures of sin, esteeming the reproach of Christ greater riches than the treasures in Egypt; for he looked to the reward [inheritance] (Hebrews 11:24–26).

David was considered to be illegitimate or, at the least, rejected by the family by many scholars, but David had the insight of the kingdom. When he fought Goliath, there was a key to David's victory. Goliath asked for a man to fight, David showed up as a Spirit Son and kicked his butt. David wrote in Psalms, "Do not take Your Holy Spirit from me," a thousand years before the veil was torn and the Holy Spirit released. But his hands were too bloody to build the temple.

Joseph was sold as a slave and helped recover the family inheritance but was willing to lay his life down for his family. He received a robe and ring but never sandals. He died a slave and reproduced who he was and enslaved the whole nation of Egypt where Pharaoh owned everything. However, his two sons, Ephraim and Manasseh, were listed with the twelve tribes of Israel, and a double portion was released.

Moses took off his sandals at the burning bush. He was doing what Boaz did to redeem Elimelech and Naomi's lost inheritance. They had been looking for the true inheritance: His presence.

> Then Boaz said, "On the day you buy the field from the hand of Naomi, you must also buy it from Ruth the Moabitess, the wife of the dead, to perpetuate the name of the dead through his inheritance." And the close relative said, "I cannot redeem it for myself, lest I ruin my own inheritance. You redeem my right of redemption for yourself, for I cannot redeem it." Now this was the custom in former times in Israel concerning redeeming and exchanging, to confirm anything: one man took off his sandal and gave it to the other, and this was a confirmation in Israel (Ruth 4:5–7).

Judah and Tamar: In Genesis 38 Tamar was looking for her inheritance; Onan only stimulated Tamar and didn't impregnate her because he spilled the kingdom seed on the ground. And God killed Onan for his disrespect of kingdom seed. The church has been good at stimulation, but she later found out that Judah was still cheating her out of her inheritance. She dressed as a harlot and received the kingdom seed that is listed in the lineage of Jesus in Mathew 1:2.

Conclusion: The Power of Redeemed Orphans!

Boaz was the kinsman redeemer. The son of Rahab the harlot, he redeemed an inheritance for Ruth and Naomi.

There is a release of the presence of the Father coming on the earth; it is going to feed the prodigals a meal that will drive them back to the Father. Sons will be granted the robe, ring, and SANDALS, but it's the party at the burning bush that recovers the lost identity.

We can't miss the burning bush experiences that will give us an opportunity to remove our sandals, and then have God remove His, and hear Him say "walk this way" in My shoes and redeem the harlots, orphans, rejected and those still entangled with the bastard curse.

The eleventh-hour workers are coming, searching for their inheritance. God is going to give Himself to them, and they will become sons of God. God started with a family, and He will redeem us as a family because that's what Fathers do.

I hope my journey will help you begin to find your true inheritance.

Blessings,

Charles L. Coker Jr.

About the Author

Charlie and Susie Coker are founders of Identity Church in Deltona, Florida. They have also been in the lighting business for over forty years, concurrently pastoring and traveling in an itinerate ministry role, releasing the light of the Father's glory. They have been married for thirty-nine years and have two sons, Jason and Bryan, and five grandchildren.

Charlie and Susie have a unique ability to share the love of God and His healing power because they have walked through the restoration of a broken marriage and broken lives. They started as orphans, dependent on self-works for God's approval, and transitioned into sons of the Father. The guidance of Jack Taylor, their spiritual father, has been vital for this process. They are transparent about their struggles, and bring healing in many areas. Because of the training of the last twenty-five years, they are able to teach others how to rule and reign from a heavenly position.

Charlie's perspective and pursuit of the kingdom of God started in 1993 when King Jesus came to personally visit him. Jesus walked the room through a wall, asked Charlie to put his hand in His hand, and assured him that He would never leave or forsake him; telling Charlie that otherwise He was going to let hell have its way with him. This introduction to the King and His kingdom gives Charlie a unique insight into how the kingdom of God functions.

Charlie can be contacted at Charlie@charliecoker.com or by visiting www.charliecoker.com.

www.ingramcontent.com/pod-product-compliance
Lightning Source LLC
Chambersburg PA
CBHW052021070526
44584CB00016B/1841